THE REVISED VERSION
EDITED FOR THE USE OF SCHOOLS

T0381939

THE

SECOND BOOK OF KINGS

THE
SECOND BOOK OF KINGS

BY

G. H. BOX, M.A.
LECTURER IN RABBINICAL HEBREW, KING'S COLLEGE, LONDON

Cambridge:
at the University Press
1914

CAMBRIDGE
UNIVERSITY PRESS

University Printing House, Cambridge CB2 8BS, United Kingdom

Published in the United States of America by Cambridge University Press, New York

Cambridge University Press is part of the University of Cambridge.

It furthers the University's mission by disseminating knowledge in the pursuit of education, learning and research at the highest international levels of excellence.

www.cambridge.org
Information on this title: www.cambridge.org/9781107663480

© Cambridge University Press 1914

First published 1914
First paperback edition 2014

A catalogue record for this publication is available from the British Library

ISBN 978-1-107-66348-0 Paperback

PREFACE BY THE GENERAL EDITOR
FOR THE OLD TESTAMENT

THE aim of this series of commentaries is to explain the Revised Version for young students, and at the same time to present, in a simple form, the main results of the best scholarship of the day.

The General Editor has confined himself to supervision and suggestion. The writer is, in each case, responsible for the opinions expressed and for the treatment of particular passages.

A. H. McNEILE.

January, 1914.

CONTENTS

MAP

INTRODUCTION[1]

§ 1. HEBREW HISTORICAL WRITINGS.

IN order to be able to appreciate the value and signifi-
cance of the historical books of the Old Testament it is
necessary to remember some facts which have an important bearing on the subject generally.

(i) These books belong to ancient—not modern—
historical literature, and must be judged accordingly.
Ancient historical works fall mainly into two classes :
they are either purely narrative in character, or invested
with a large didactic element.

(ii) The historical books of the O.T. belong to the
latter class. Though they contain large masses of
narrative—often of unsurpassed power and beauty[2]—
they are, on the whole, examples of *history written with
a purpose*. The aim of the writers is to inculcate and
illustrate certain lessons of a religious character, or
certain religious ideas, specially dear to particular schools
of religious thought. The material embodied in their
work has, therefore, been selected and treated in accordance with this special purpose.

(iii) The historical literature of the O.T. is mainly the
work of two schools of writers which may be named
respectively the *prophetic* and the *priestly*. The Books

---

[1] 1 and 2 Kings form two divisions of a single work. The
division between them is purely arbitrary. For the title and
place of the Book in the Canon see the Introduction to 1 Kings
in this Series, § 1.

[2] e.g. the history of Joseph, and the David-narratives.

of Kings belong to the former class. During the Exile, a school of writers, under the influence of Deuteronomy —a book which largely embodies the ideas of the prophetic party—completed the compilation of a comprehensive historical work which surveyed the entire history from the Creation down to the destruction of Jerusalem, and included a notice of the release of King Jehoiachin from imprisonment in 562 B.C. This work—which was essentially a compilation, embodying large excerpts from earlier sources fitted together in an editorial framework— consisted of the narrative part of the Hexateuch known as JE[1], together with a form of Deuteronomy, and the greater part of the Books of Judges, Samuel, and Kings, as we have them. Later, another comprehensive historical work was compiled by the Chronicler (about 250 B.C.). This surveyed the history, from Adam to Nehemiah, from the priestly standpoint, and is contained in the Books of Chronicles and Ezra-Nehemiah.

§ 2. THE AUTHORSHIP AND DATE OF 2 KINGS.

The place and general character of 2 Kings in this literature will thus be clear. It is essentially a compilation, based largely upon earlier sources—but a compilation which has had a strongly marked character impressed upon it by the compiler.

It is now generally held that the Books of Kings owe their present shape to the work of two Deuteronomic editors (sometimes referred to as D[1], D[2]). The earlier of these may be regarded as the real author. 'He was imbued with the spirit of Deuteronomy, and wrote in the later days of the Judaean monarchy, perhaps in the reign of Jehoiakim (c. 600 B.C.). To him must be ascribed the characteristic scheme for the survey of each royal

---

[1] i.e. the Jahvistic and Elohistic parts of Genesis, Exodus, Numbers and Joshua. For details see the various *Introductions* to the Literature of the O.T.

reign which runs through the whole book[1].' This compiler may be regarded as the author of 1 Kings i.—2 Kings xxiv. (apart from some later elements) in the sense that he collected and selected the great mass of the material, and gave it its present shape.

A later editor of the same school, who must have written in the latter half of the Babylonian Exile, completed the work by bringing the history down to the Exile, and at the same time interpolated a few passages, which were designed to show that the final ruin of the Judaean state was rendered inevitable by idolatry.

§ 3. THE SOURCES OF 2 KINGS.

It has already been stated that the compiler utilized much older material, which, in various degrees, he has embodied in his work. That he consulted ancient authorities is clear from his own explicit statements. He constantly refers his readers for further information regarding the secular affairs of various reigns to certain chronicles—for the Northern Kingdom 'the Book of the Annals of the Kings of Israel,' and for the Southern 'the Book of the Annals of the Kings of Judah[2].' These 'Annals' were themselves probably continuous historical works, based upon the state archives. But, further, it may be inferred with tolerable certainty that the compiler has utilized other sources as well—in particular, the great

---

[1] This is what is meant by the 'framework.' It is marked by a stereotyped formula—in the case of the Judaean kings, the age of each on ascending the throne is given, the duration of his reign, the name of his mother, his death and burial; in the case of the Israelite kings, merely the length of the reign and the king's death. See my *Short Introd. to Lit. of O.T.* p. 78 f. The compiler's work increases in extent as the narrative approaches his own times. Thus ch. xxi. (Manasseh) and xxii. 1—xxiii. 30 (Josiah's Reformation) are largely his work.
[2] The regular formula is: '*Now the rest of the acts of...are they not written in the Book of the Annals of the Kings of Israel (Judah)?*'

collection of Elijah and Elisha narratives[1] appear to be based upon cycles of prophetic biographies, and stories, probably of North Israelitish origin. These were, perhaps, embodied in more than one work (cf. introductory note on i. 2—17a)[2]. Another source may have been a 'Temple-history,' based upon the Temple-archives (cf. the introductory notes on xii. 4—16, xvi. 10—16, and xxii.—xxiii. 22). In xxiii. 16—20 a late Midrashic[3] work seems to have been drawn upon, which is also probably the source of 1 Kings xiii. 1 f. Finally the long passage xviii. 17—xx. 10 (= Isaiah xxxvi.—xxxix.) is derived from a biography of Isaiah which not improbably is to be identified with *the vision of Isaiah* referred to in 2 Chron. xxxii. 32 (see the introductory note to xviii.—xxv.).

§ 4. THE CHRONOLOGY.

One of the most striking features of *Kings* is the elaborate series of chronological statements contained in the framework. It will be impossible here, however, to enter into a full discussion of the intricate questions involved in the system as a whole[4]. One or two points can, however, be noted. It will be observed that the chronological *data* of the framework are of two kinds : the length of the reigns is given, and (for the period of the

---

[1] Appearing in 1 Kings xvii.—xix., xxi. and 2 Kings i. 2 f., ii., iv.—vi., viii. and xiii.

[2] See further my *Short Introd. to Lit. of O.T.* p. 81 f.

[3] 'The Midrash may be defined as an imaginative development of a thought or theme suggested by Scripture, especially a didactic or homiletic exposition or an edifying religious story.' This branch of literature has undergone a rich development in Rabbinical Judaism. The word *midrash* means literally *investigation*. It occurs for the first time in 2 Chron. xiii. 22 and xxiv. 27. See further my *Short Introd. to Lit. of O.T.* p. 88.

[4] Fuller information must be sought in the Commentaries and Bible Dictionaries.

divided kingdom) a number of synchronisms[1]. The latter
are often beset with great difficulties, and are sometimes
mutually irreconcileable (cf. e.g. xviii. 9 and 14). On the
whole, it is safer to ignore the synchronisms, as probably
due to (later) editorial calculation, and to direct attention
primarily to the statements as to the length of the reigns,
which are probably derived ultimately from state records.
Here an important question arises as to the method of
calculating the length of each reign. There is some
reason to suppose that the year in which one reign ended
and another began was reckoned *twice*; it was counted
as a full year to the reign of the deceased king, and also
as a full year to his successor. If this be so, it will be
necessary to deduct from the sum of the reigns one year
for each reign in order to arrive at a correct result. This
method is helpful in fixing the year of Hezekiah's accession, one of the points of difficulty. Did the fall of
Samaria—the date of which is fixed by Assyrian evidence
as 722—take place in the sixth year of Hezekiah (2 Kings
xviii. 10), or, as some scholars maintain, in the latter
part of the reign of Ahaz? The sum of the reigns from
the accession of Hezekiah to Zedekiah is 140 years;
deducting 7 we get 133 years, and reckoning backwards
from the destruction of Jerusalem in 587 B.C. we arrive,
on this *datum*, at 720 B.C. as the accession-year of
Hezekiah (587 + 133 = 720), which is probably correct.
Another serious difficulty arises in connexion with the
period from the revolution of Jehu to the fall of Samaria.
Here the sum of the Israelitish reigns is 144, and of the
Judaean 165 years; if we deduct one year from each reign,
the figures are 135 and 158 respectively. How is the
discrepancy to be explained? There is an obvious

---

[1] A 'synchronism' denotes the occurrence of an event at the
same time as some other event; cf. e.g. 2 Kings viii. 25: *In
the twelfth year of Joram the son of Ahab king of Israel did
Ahaziah the son of Jehoram king of Judah begin to reign.*

difficulty in connexion with the reign of Azariah (Uzziah) of Judah (cf. note on xv. 1). The best solution is that of Rost, who proposes to reduce the reign of Amaziah of Judah from 29 to 9 years (cf. xiv. 2), and to regard the greater part of the 16 years assigned to Jotham (cf. xv. 53) as included in his regency (cf. xv. 5), he having ruled only 5 years independently.

With these adjustments the following chronological scheme results (for the reigns included in 2 Kings):

ISRAEL AND JUDAH

JUDAH

Length of reign: years						Date of accession
8	Jehoram	...	..	...	...	850
1	Ahaziah	...	...	...	...	843
7	Athaliah	...	...	...	...	843
40	Jehoash	...	...	...	...	837
9	Amaziah	...	...	...	...	798
52	{ Azariah (Uzziah)		...	...	...	790
	{ Jotham (regent)		...	...	...	749
5	Jotham (alone) ...		...	...	...	739
16	Ahaz	...	...	...	...	735

ISRAEL

Length of reign: years						Date of accession
2	Ahaziah	...	...	...	...	855
12	Jehoram	...	...	...	...	854
28	Jehu	...	...	...	...	843
17	Jehoahaz	...	...	...	...	816
16	Jehoash	...	...	...	...	800
41	Jeroboam II	...	...	...	...	785
7 months	Zechariah, Shallum	...	...	...	745
10 years	Menahem	...	...	...	...	745
2	Pekahiah	...	...	...	...	736
4	Pekah	...	...	...	...	735
11	Hosea	...	...	...	...	732
	Fall of Samaria (end of N. Kingdom)					722

JUDAH ALONE

Length of reign: years				Date of accession
29	Hezekiah	...	...	720
55	Manasseh	...	...	692
2	Amon ...	...	...	638
31	Josiah ...	...	...	637
3 months	Jehoahaz ...	...	...	607
11 years	Jehoiakim	...	...	607
3 months	Jehoiachin	...	...	597 (First Captivity)
11 years	Zedekiah ...	...	...	597

Fall of Jerusalem, 587.

The following dates are fixed by the monuments:

Jehu's tribute to Assyria, 842.

Menahem pays tribute to Assyria, 738.

Galilee devastated by Tiglath-Pileser, 733.

Assyrians capture Damascus, 732.

Sennacherib's campaign against Judah, 701.

Battle of Carchemish, 605.

ABBREVIATIONS

LXX = the Septuagint, i.e. the Greek Version.

LXX (Luc.) = the Lucianic Recension of the LXX, i.e. the edition of the LXX made by Lucian of Antioch (died 312 A.D.). This preserves many valuable old readings otherwise unknown.

D^1 = the original Deuteronomic editor of *Kings*.

D^2 = the younger (Exilic) Deuteronomic editor of *Kings*.

O.T. = Old Testament.

THE
SECOND BOOK OF KINGS

I. THE REIGN OF AHAZIAH, KING OF ISRAEL, CONTINUED.

i. 1. *A notice about the rebellion of Moab.*

AND Moab rebelled against Israel after the death of 1 Ahab.

i. 2–17 a. *The death of Ahaziah predicted by Elijah.*

And Ahaziah fell down through the lattice in his upper 2 chamber that was in Samaria, and was sick: and he sent

---

i. 1. The division of the original Book of Kings at this point is purely arbitrary, and occurs in the middle of the account of a reign, viz. that of Ahaziah, son of Ahab, the former part of which is given in 1 Kings xxii. 51–53.

1. Moab rebelled against Israel: a fuller account of this rebellion is given in iii. 4 foll. See notes there.

2–17 a. The following section belongs to the cycle of biographical narratives which are concerned with the life of Elijah, extracts from which have already appeared in 1 Kings xvii.–xix., xxi. Another cycle, which we shall meet with in the following chapters (ii., iv.–vi., viii., xiii.), illustrates the life of Elisha. The prophetic biographies from which these extracts are taken were among the sources used by the compiler of the book. See *Introd.* § 3. The story here narrated gives the occasion of the great prophet's last public appearance as the champion and upholder of the religion of Jehovah.

2. through the lattice in his upper chamber: ordinary houses were one storey high, and on the flat roof of such it was not unusual for an upper room to be erected (cf. iv. 10). A royal palace, however, would be built on a larger scale, and 'the upper chamber' on its roof from which Ahaziah fell may have been several storeys high. The opening which served as a window was protected by a **lattice** (lit. 'network'). It was through this opening that the king—perhaps as he was leaning out—fell, probably into the courtyard below.

messengers, and said unto them, Go, inquire of Baal-zebub
the god of Ekron whether I shall recover of this sickness.
3 But the angel of the LORD said to Elijah the Tishbite,
Arise, go up to meet the messengers of the king of
Samaria, and say unto them, Is it because there is no
God in Israel, that ye go to inquire of Baal-zebub the
4 god of Ekron? Now therefore thus saith the LORD,

Baal-zebub the god of Ekron: the name **Baal-zebub**, according to the traditional explanation, means 'Lord (or Baal) of flies,'
i.e. probably a god who both sends and removes a plague of flies.
But the worship of such a god among the Semites is not certainly
referred to elsewhere, and is highly doubtful.   Another explanation is that **zebub** is an ancient place-name; but in that case
Baal-zebub could not very well be called **the god of Ekron**.
Perhaps it is an alteration (or corruption) of *Baal-zebul* 'Lord of
the high house,' which may have been given as a title of honour
to the god of Ekron, and also to other gods; compare Beelzebul
(Matt. x. 25 *R.V. marg.*), which is, apparently, the correct form
in the Gospels where it is used as the name of an evil spirit (spelt
in some MSS Beelzebub).

Ekron: of the five chief Philistine cities (Gaza, Ashkelon,
Ashdod, Ekron, and Gath) Ekron was the one that lay nearest
to Judah.   It is identified with the modern *'Akir*, south-west of
er-Ramleh, and about nine miles from the coast.

3.   the angel of the Lord: the angel of the Lord (i.e. of
Jehovah) is often the medium by whom Jehovah, especially in
some of the older narratives (JE) which deal with the patriarchs,
conveyed His will.   In fact he may be regarded as a visible
manifestation of Jehovah Himself, in those narratives.   So possibly
here (contrast xix. 35 where the expression probably denotes a
creature-angel distinct from Jehovah, as in 2 Sam. xxiv. 16).
In the other Elijah-narratives, the phrase used is: 'And the
word of the Lord came [to Elijah],' e.g. 1 Kings xvii. 3.   In
2 Kings xix. 35 'the angel of the Lord' appears as the instrument
of the divine vengeance on the Assyrians.

Elijah the Tishbite: Elijah was of *Tisbe* (or *Thisbe*) *in
Gilead*, according to 1 Kings xvii. 1 (as the LXX understands
the text there), a locality to be distinguished from the Galilean
Tisbe (Tobit i. 2); but its exact position is unknown.

the king of Samaria: not 'king of Israel'—the expression is
slightly contemptuous.

Is it because etc.: no rival worship would be tolerated by
the God of Israel.   A feeling of fierce indignation was roused in
the prophet by Ahaziah's readiness to resort to a foreign god.

Thou shalt not come down from the bed whither thou
art gone up, but shalt surely die. And Elijah departed.
And the messengers returned unto him, and he said unto 5
them, Why is it that ye are returned? And they said 6
unto him, There came up a man to meet us, and said
unto us, Go, turn again unto the king that sent you, and
say unto him, Thus saith the LORD, Is it because there
is no God in Israel, that thou sendest to inquire of Baal-
zebub the god of Ekron? therefore thou shalt not come
down from the bed whither thou art gone up, but shalt
surely die. And he said unto them, What manner of 7
man was he which came up to meet you, and told you
these words? And they answered him, He was an hairy 8
man, and girt with a girdle of leather about his loins.
And he said, It is Elijah the Tishbite. Then *the king* 9
sent unto him a captain of fifty with his fifty. And he
went up to him: and, behold, he sat on the top of the
hill. And he spake unto him, O man of God, the king
hath said, Come down. And Elijah answered and said 10

---

8. He was an hairy man etc.: lit. 'a possessor of hair,' i.e.
clothed with a hairy garment. The mantle of skin covered with
hair is referred to, which already, in the time of Elijah, was a
mark of the prophetic office (cf. 1 Kings xix. 19), as it was also
in later times, cf. Zech. xiii. 4 ('neither shall they wear a hairy
mantle to deceive'); Matt. iii. 4 (of John the Baptist). Such
dress is of the simplest kind; a sheep or a goat's skin, with the
hair left on, is still commonly worn by the Bedawis. For the
girdle (lit. 'waistcloth') **of leather** (not mentioned again in the
O.T.) cf. Mark i. 6.

9 ff. It is difficult to reconcile the painful episode of Elijah's
calling down fire from heaven, described in the following verses,
with the picture of the prophet given in 1 Kings xvii.–xix., and
xxi. In the latter chapters Elijah stands out as a man of God
of supreme moral greatness and power. Probably the story
given in these verses was derived from popular tradition, and is
merely a naive expression of the immense impression made by
the prophet's personality upon the popular imagination. It
depicts the prophet as asserting his powers as a man of God.

9. on the top of the hill: what hill is not specified.

to the captain of fifty, If I be a man of God, let fire come
down from heaven, and consume thee and thy fifty. And
there came down fire from heaven, and consumed him
11 and his fifty. And again he sent unto him another
captain of fifty with his fifty. And he answered and
said unto him, O man of God, thus hath the king said,
12 Come down quickly. And Elijah answered and said
unto them, If I be a man of God, let fire come down
from heaven, and consume thee and thy fifty. And the
fire of God came down from heaven, and consumed him
13 and his fifty. And again he sent the captain of a third
fifty with his fifty. And the third captain of fifty went
up, and came and fell on his knees before Elijah, and
besought him, and said unto him, O man of God, I pray
thee, let my life, and the life of these fifty thy servants, be
14 precious in thy sight. Behold, there came fire down
from heaven, and consumed the two former captains of
fifty with their fifties: but now let my life be precious in
15 thy sight. And the angel of the LORD said unto Elijah,
Go down with him: be not afraid of him. And he
16 arose, and went down with him unto the king. And he
said unto him, Thus saith the LORD, Forasmuch as thou
hast sent messengers to inquire of Baal-zebub the god of

---

10. If I be a man of God etc.: in reply to the insulting
summons the prophet demonstrates, by supernatural means, the
reality of his claim to be a 'man of God.' The mere fact that
the king had despatched soldiers to bring in Elijah shows that
he was animated by hostile intentions.

11. And he answered: read 'and he went up,' as in *vv.* 9
and 13; so the best text of the LXX.

13. the captain of a third fifty: read with LXX (Luc.) and
other authorities 'a third captain of fifty.'

fell on his knees before Elijah: the humble demeanour of
this 'captain' contrasts forcibly with the attitude of the former
officers. This one shows proper respect to the man of God.
In this feature the main point and moral of the story seem to
lie. It should be noted that the military forces of Israel were
organized by thousands, hundreds, and fifties; each of these had
its 'captain' (Heb. *sar*): cf. Numb. xxxi. 14, 18; 1 Sam. vii. 12.

Ekron, is it because there is no God in Israel to inquire
of his word? therefore thou shalt not come down from the
bed whither thou art gone up, but shalt surely die. So he 17
died according to the word of the LORD which Elijah
had spoken.

i. 17 b, 18. *Concluding notice of Ahaziah's reign.*

And Jehoram began to reign in his stead in the second
year of Jehoram the son of Jehoshaphat king of Judah;
because he had no son.   Now the rest of the acts of 18
Ahaziah which he did, are they not written in the book of
the chronicles of the kings of Israel?

II. ELISHA SUCCEEDS ELIJAH.

ii. 1–18. *Elijah translated to heaven.*

And it came to pass, when the LORD would take up 2
Elijah by a whirlwind into heaven, that Elijah went with

---

16. is it because...word? These words are rightly omitted
by the LXX; they are a gloss from *vv.* 3 and 6.

17 b, 18. There are several peculiarities in this concluding
formula. Clearly *v.* 17 *b* is out of place, it should be preceded
by *v.* 18, which should itself be preceded by a notice of the
king's burial. Then, again, the synchronism 'in the second year
of Jehoram' is difficult. It belongs to a different system of
chronology from that otherwise employed in the book. The
text is obviously in disorder, as the variations in the LXX MSS
show. Probably the confusion is due to displacements which
have resulted from editorial revision.

17. And Jehoram: the LXX (B) adds 'son of Ahab' (but
LXX (Luc.) 'his brother'—rightly).

in the second year of Jehoram...Judah: according to iii. 4
this should be 'in the eighteenth year of Jehoshaphat king of
Judah.' LXX (Luc.) combines both synchronisms.

18. This *v.* rightly follows 17 *a* in the ordinary text of the
LXX, which continues with a notice of Jehoram's succession
identical with that which we have in iii. 1–4.

ii. 1–18. With chapter ii. begins a series of narratives which
have Elisha as their central figure (ii., iv.–vii., viii. 1–15, and
xiii. 14–21). Like the parallel series which is concerned with
Elijah they appear to have been extracted from a biography of
Elisha, containing traditions and stories about the prophet and
his work, which had probably been collected and written down
before the Book of Kings was compiled. The collection and

2 Elisha from Gilgal. And Elijah said unto Elisha, Tarry
here, I pray thee; for the LORD hath sent me as far as
Beth-el. And Elisha said, As the LORD liveth, and as
thy soul liveth, I will not leave thee. So they went down
3 to Beth-el. And the sons of the prophets that were at

---

writing down of the narratives was probably carried out in the
prophetic circles, by 'the sons of the prophets.' The narratives,
as a whole, doubtless give a faithful picture of the general
character of Elisha's life and activities, which moved on a lower
plane than his great predecessor's.

The account of Elijah's translation to heaven which follows is
to be regarded as the introduction to the Elisha-cycle. Its central
point is the description of the manner in which the succession
passed from Elijah to Elisha. This is represented as a matter of
uncertainty, up to the last, to Elijah himself, who makes it conditional upon Elisha's ability to perceive, in spiritual vision, the
departure of his master to heaven. In the event Elisha responds
to the test, and invests himself with the mantle and authority of
Elijah, being recognized also as Elijah's successor by 'the sons
of the prophets.' It should be noticed, however, that according
to the Elijah-cycle of biographic narratives, Elisha had already
been designated by Elijah, during the latter's active ministry,
as his successor, and invested with the prophetic mantle (cf.
1 Kings xix.).

1. from Gilgal: Gilgal (=[*sacred*] *circle* [*of stones*]) was the
name of several places in Israel, to which such a name would
naturally apply from the survival of sacred stones or cromlechs.
The Gilgal here intended appears to have been the usual place
of residence, or resort, of both Elijah and Elisha, and was the
seat of a prophetic community (cf. iv. 38 and notes). It has been
plausibly identified with the modern *Jiljilie*, about seven miles
north of Bethel, with which it is closely connected as a sanctuary
by Amos and Hosea (cf. Amos iv. 4; Hosea iv. 15). It stands
on high ground in the hill-country of Ephraim (notice in *v.* 2
Elijah and Elisha 'go down' to Bethel), and commands a wide
view over the whole country. Both Bethel and Gilgal were seats
of the old (pagan) Canaanitish worship, and also of prophetic
guilds (or communities of 'the sons of the prophets').

3. the sons of the prophets: i.e. members of the prophetic
guilds; 'son,' in this connexion, has this meaning simply, so that
an individual member of such a guild could be called a 'prophet'
(cf. ix. 4) or 'son of a prophet' (cf. Amos vii. 14, 'I was (am) no
prophet, neither...a prophet's son'). It is noteworthy that the
prophetic gift is associated, in some of its earliest recorded manifestations, with companies or 'bands' of prophets (cf. 1 Sam.

Beth-el came forth to Elisha, and said unto him, Knowest
thou that the LORD will take away thy master from thy
head to-day?   And he said, Yea, I know it; hold ye your
peace.   And Elijah said unto him, Elisha, tarry here, 4
I pray thee; for the LORD hath sent me to Jericho.   And
he said, As the LORD liveth, and as thy soul liveth,
I will not leave thee.   So they came to Jericho.   And 5
the sons of the prophets that were at Jericho came near
to Elisha, and said unto him, Knowest thou that the
LORD will take away thy master from thy head to-day?

---

x. 10 f., 'behold a band of prophets met him' etc.; xix. 20 f.),
which probably, in the time of Samuel, played an important
part in rousing the national patriotic spirit against foreign
(Philistine) oppression.   Apparently between the times of
Samuel and Elisha these prophetic communities had been
strengthened in their organization—perhaps, the initiative came
from Samuel himself—and placed upon a more definite and
stricter basis.   At any rate they appear, in the history of Elisha,
as definitely organized communities, with fixed settlements; here
they lived a common life (cf. iv. 38 f.; vi. 1 f., 'the place where
we dwell' etc.), though not as celibates (cf. iv. 1 f.), and were
(in part at any rate) supported by charitable gifts (cf. iv. 42, v. 22).
They cultivated music and song (cf. 1 Sam. x. 5; 2 Kings iii. 15),
and it is possible that they helped to preserve and develope the
patriotic ballad poetry of the nation.   Though in the Elisha-
narratives the prophet himself appears as their acknowledged
head, it must not be supposed that the communities of 'the sons
of the prophets' are to be regarded as Elisha's personal disciples.
They were essentially independent bodies, professional in character,
and by no means always animated by the higher ideals.   It is
significant that four hundred prophets of Jehovah could be relied
upon by Ahab to bless his expedition to Ramoth-Gilead (1 Kings
xxii. 6).

4.   Jericho: the site of the ancient city (which has been the
scene of some recent excavations) is near the modern village of
er-Riha, about five miles from the north end of the Dead Sea,
in the Jordan valley.   The ancient site is represented by a number
of mounds beside a spring traditionally associated with Elisha
(see *v.* 19 note).   For the tradition of the rebuilding of Jericho
cf. 1 Kings xvi. 34.

5.   from thy head to-day (also *v.* 3): i.e. from over thy head:
Elijah occupied the position of supreme authority as the master
and teacher of Elisha: **to-day** is emphatic.

And he answered, Yea, I know it; hold ye your peace.
6 And Elijah said unto him, Tarry here, I pray thee; for
the LORD hath sent me to Jordan. And he said, As the
LORD liveth, and as thy soul liveth, I will not leave thee.
7 And they two went on. And fifty men of the sons of the
prophets went, and stood over against them afar off: and
8 they two stood by Jordan. And Elijah took his mantle,
and wrapped it together, and smote the waters, and they
were divided hither and thither, so that they two went
9 over on dry ground. And it came to pass, when they
were gone over, that Elijah said unto Elisha, Ask what
I shall do for thee, before I be taken from thee. And
Elisha said, I pray thee, let a double portion of thy spirit
10 be upon me. And he said, Thou hast asked a hard
thing: *nevertheless*, if thou see me when I am taken

---

6. to Jordan: Jericho was a short distance from the river.

7. fifty men of the sons of the prophets: the double
miracle of the division of the waters of the river, where there
was no ford, was effected in the presence of fifty witnesses (cf.
v. 15).

stood over against them afar off: i.e. directly opposite the
spot where they were standing (by the brink of the river), but at
some distance inland.

8. his mantle: i.e. the mantle of hair, which was the dis-
tinguishing dress of the prophet: cf. i. 8 and notes. It is by this
mantle, which has passed to him from his master, that Elisha
repeats the miracle of the division of the waters (cf. *v.* 14). For
the idea of power inhering in the garments of a great personality,
cf. Mark v. 28 ff. (esp. *v.* 30); see also Ezek. xliv. 19.

9. a double portion: by the Mosaic Law the firstborn son
inherited two parts of his father's property (cf. Deut. xxi. 17,
'a double portion of all that he hath'). So here Elisha asks that
he may be treated as a firstborn son among the disciples of Elijah,
inheriting a share twice as large as any passing to the others, of
his master's spirit. His request amounts to a petition that he
may succeed his master as head of all the prophets.

10. if thou see me etc.: the faculty for seeing heavenly
realities is not granted to every man (cf. vi. 17). If in the event
Elisha is found to possess such a gift he will know that his prayer
has been answered.

from thee, it shall be so unto thee; but if not, it shall
not be so. And it came to pass, as they still went on, 11
and talked, that, behold, *there appeared* a chariot of fire,
and horses of fire, which parted them both asunder; and
Elijah went up by a whirlwind into heaven. And Elisha 12
saw it, and he cried, My father, my father, the chariots of
Israel and the horsemen thereof! And he saw him no
more: and he took hold of his own clothes, and rent
them in two pieces. He took up also the mantle of Elijah 13
that fell from him, and went back, and stood by the bank
of Jordan. And he took the mantle of Elijah that fell 14
from him, and smote the waters, and said, Where is the
LORD, the God of Elijah? and when he also had smitten

---

11. a chariot of fire: or, perhaps, 'chariots' (the Heb. word
employed is usually collective in meaning): cf. vi. 17 ('horses
and chariots of fire round about Elisha'). As the divine title
'Jehovah of Hosts' shows, the God of Israel was conceived as
accompanied by a heavenly army, a natural accompaniment of
which would be heavenly chariots; cf. Ps. lxviii. 17 ('The chariots
of God are twenty thousand' etc.); Hab. iii. 8 ('Thou didst ride
upon Thy horses, Thy chariots of salvation'). Such chariots,
normally invisible to mortal eyes, are only visible to those of the
enlightened (cf. vi. 17); and so here the 'chariots of fire' which
carried Elijah to heaven were not visible to the fifty 'sons of the
prophets,' who only after a three days' search were convinced of
the prophet's departure from earth (cf. *v.* 16).

Elijah went up by a whirlwind into heaven: or, rather, 'went
up in the storm heavenward': Jehovah, according to Hebrew
ideas, was present and displayed His power in the convulsions
and activities of nature (the storm, clouds, lightning: cf. Ps.
xviii. 10 f.); so the literal meaning of the present passage must
not be unduly pressed: it describes, with poetical vividness, how
'God suddenly took Elijah to Himself, amid a grand display of
His power in and through the forces of nature' (Ball).

12. the chariots of Israel and the horsemen thereof: in
xiii. 14 these words are applied to Elisha. In both cases the
meaning is that the prophet is a source of strength to his people,
worth all its material horses and chariots.

14. Where is the Lord, the God of Elijah? The question
means: 'Jehovah has not departed from the earth with His
prophet: in order to make this clear to all, let Him now show

the waters, they were divided hither and thither: and
15 Elisha went over. And when the sons of the prophets
which were at Jericho over against him saw him, they
said, The spirit of Elijah doth rest on Elisha. And they
came to meet him, and bowed themselves to the ground
16 before him. And they said unto him, Behold now, there
be with thy servants fifty strong men; let them go, we
pray thee, and seek thy master: lest peradventure the
spirit of the LORD hath taken him up, and cast him upon
some mountain, or into some valley. And he said, Ye
17 shall not send. And when they urged him till he was
ashamed, he said, Send. They sent therefore fifty men;
18 and they sought three days, but found him not. And
they came back to him, while he tarried at Jericho; and
he said unto them, Did I not say unto you, Go not?

ii. 19-22. *The unwholesome waters healed.*

19   And the men of the city said unto Elisha, Behold,
we pray thee, the situation of this city is pleasant, as
my lord seeth: but the water is naught, and the land

His power through me, and at the same time demonstrate that
the powers wielded by Elijah are now at my command.'
     he also should be omitted—there is an error in the Hebrew
text.
     15. which were at Jericho: these words are probably an
incorrect addition to the original text (cf. *v.* 7), and should be
omitted.
     The spirit of Elijah: i.e. the divine spirit which worked in
Elijah, and manifested itself in wonder-working power.
     **16. the spirit of the Lord hath taken him up...upon some
mountain**: cf. 1 Kings xviii. 12; Acts viii. 39, 40. Elijah's
sudden appearances and disappearances had suggested that he
was carried hither and thither by the spirit of Jehovah. The
prophets now urge that his last disappearance may be accounted
for in the same way, and he may still be found alive somewhere.
The fruitless search confirms the truth of Elisha's vision.
     19. the city: Jericho is meant.
     the water is naught: or, rather, 'bad': a spring known as '*Ain
es-Sultân*, which rises beside the mounds that mark the ancient
city of Jericho, is traditionally associated with Elisha. It is still

miscarrieth. And he said, Bring me a new cruse, and put 20
salt therein. And they brought it to him. And he went 21
forth unto the spring of the waters, and cast salt therein,
and said, Thus saith the LORD, I have healed these
waters; there shall not be from thence any more death or
miscarrying. So the waters were healed unto this day, 22
according to the word of Elisha which he spake.

ii. 23–25. *Elisha and the insulting 'children' of Bethel.*

And he went up from thence unto Beth-el: and as he 23
was going up by the way, there came forth little children
out of the city, and mocked him, and said unto him, Go
up, thou bald head; go up, thou bald head. And he 24
looked behind him and saw them, and cursed them in the
name of the LORD. And there came forth two she-bears
out of the wood, and tare forty and two children of them.
And he went from thence to mount Carmel, and from 25
thence he returned to Samaria.

III. THE REIGN OF JEHORAM OF ISRAEL; HIS CAMPAIGN AGAINST MOAB.

iii. 1–3. *Introduction.*

Now Jehoram the son of Ahab began to reign over 3

---

a perennial fountain of sweet water, and is doubtless the fountain
referred to here. The passage reflects the local tradition.

the land miscarrieth: i.e. causes miscarriages or abortions:
R.V. marg. 'casteth her fruit' is less likely.

22. unto this day: this phrase suggests that when the
narrative was written, the story was already very old.

23–25. The moral intended, apparently, to be enforced by
this story is similar to that of i. 9 f., viz. that proper respect must
be paid to the office and person of Jehovah's prophet. The story
may also, perhaps, illustrate the unpopularity of Jehovah's true
prophets at Bethel, the chief centre of the calf-worship (cf. Amos
vii. 10 f.). 'Children' should be rendered 'youths.' They were
old enough to know better.

23. Go up, thou bald head: baldness was accounted a disgrace
in antiquity; cf. Is. iii. 17–24.

25. returned to Samaria: some scholars think that 'Samaria'
is a later correction of the original text, which had 'to Gilgal'
(cf. *v.* 1).

Israel in Samaria in the eighteenth year of Jehoshaphat
2 king of Judah, and reigned twelve years. And he did
that which was evil in the sight of the LORD; but not
like his father, and like his mother: for he put away the

---

iii. 1–3. The introductory verses come from the hand of the
Deuteronomic compiler. It is doubtful whether the rest of the
chapter is to be assigned to the Elisha biographical cycle of
narratives or not. The narrative may owe its place here, in the
midst of other chapters which undoubtedly belong to the Elisha-
cycle, to the fact that the central incident is connected with the
prophet (cf. *vv.* 11 f.). On the other hand it resembles in general
character the popular historical narrative, from which 1 Kings
xx., xxii. were derived.

The present chapter describes an unsuccessful expedition which
was undertaken by Jehoram of Israel and his vassal Jehoshaphat,
king of Judah, to restore the supremacy of Israel over Moab.
Mesha, king of Moab, had rebelled and refused to pay the
accustomed tribute to the king of Israel. In the famous Moabite
stone, discovered at Dibon, we have Mesha's own account of his
successful revolt. He describes how his land had been oppressed
by Omri, king of Israel, and also by the latter's son (Ahab), for
forty years, and how, in the middle of Ahab's reign by the help of
Chemosh, the Moabite god, he had driven the invaders out of his
land. According to the Biblical account, however, Mesha's rebellion only took place *after* the death of Ahab. The chronology
of the two records thus does not agree; in fact according to the
chronology of the Books of Kings the united reigns of Omri and
Ahab do not amount to forty years. In other respects the two
accounts confirm each other. Our present chapter describes
events which were subsequent to those narrated in Mesha's
inscription.

1.   in the eighteenth year of Jehoshaphat king of Judah:
this chronology, which is probably right, agrees with 1 Kings
xxii. 52, according to which passage Ahaziah 'began to reign
over Israel…in the seventeenth year of Jehoshaphat, and reigned
two years.' In 2 Kings i. 17 a different chronological scheme is
followed, according to which Jehoram of Israel began his reign
in the second year of Jehoram, son of Jehoshaphat, of Judah
(cf. also 2 Kings viii. 16).

2.   like his mother: his mother Jezebel was still alive, and
survived him (cf. ix. 30).

for he put away the pillar of Baal: i.e. from the temple of
Baal. The LXX, with some other Versions, reads 'pillars,' and
adds 'and brake them in pieces.' This may be right. Jehoram,

pillar of Baal that his father had made. Nevertheless he 3
cleaved unto the sins of Jeroboam the son of Nebat,
wherewith he made Israel to sin; he departed not therefrom.

iii. 4–10.   *Preparations for the campaign against Moab.*

Now Mesha king of Moab was a sheepmaster; and he 4
rendered unto the king of Israel the wool of an hundred
thousand lambs, and of an hundred thousand rams.
But it came to pass, when Ahab was dead, that the 5
king of Moab rebelled against the king of Israel. And 6
king Jehoram went out of Samaria at that time, and
mustered all Israel. And he went and sent to Jehosha- 7
phat the king of Judah, saying, The king of Moab hath
rebelled against me: wilt thou go with me against Moab
to battle? And he said, I will go up: I am as thou art,
my people as thy people, my horses as thy horses. And 8
he said, Which way shall we go up? And he answered,
The way of the wilderness of Edom. So the king of 9

---

however, did not destroy the worship of Baal, which still flourished
till Jehu abolished it.

3.   he cleaved unto the sins of Jeroboam: cf. 1 Kings xii.
28 f., xvi. 2, 26.

4.   a sheepmaster: the same Hebrew word (*nôqēd*) is used
to describe the occupation of the prophet Amos (Amos i. 1
'among the herdmen of Tekoa'); and in both cases a special
breed of stunted and short-legged sheep is referred to, which was
much esteemed on account of its wool. This breed is still called
by the Arabs *naqad*. Mesha was a breeder of such sheep.

he rendered: rather 'used to render,' i.e. yearly.

the wool: the rendering of the text is to be preferred to that
of the margin ('an hundred thousand lambs...with the wool').
The amount of tribute seems excessive and may be due to corruption of the text.

7.   and sent to Jehoshaphat etc.: the king of Judah is
treated as a vassal; cf. 1 Kings xxii. 4.

8.   The way of the wilderness of Edom: Moab was to be
attacked from the south (see map). Mesha, as we learn from
his inscription, had fortified the cities along his northern border,
operations along which would also be dangerous on account of
the Syrians.

Israel went, and the king of Judah, and the king of
Edom : and they made a circuit of seven days' journey :
and there was no water for the host, nor for the beasts
10 that followed them.   And the king of Israel said, Alas!
for the LORD hath called these three kings together to
deliver them into the hand of Moab.

iii. 11–20.   *Elisha consulted.*

11 But Jehoshaphat said, Is there not here a prophet of
the LORD, that we may inquire of the LORD by him?
And one of the king of Israel's servants answered and
said, Elisha the son of Shaphat is here, which poured
12 water on the hands of Elijah.   And Jehoshaphat said,
The word of the LORD is with him.   So the king of Israel
and Jehoshaphat and the king of Edom went down to
13 him.   And Elisha said unto the king of Israel, What have
I to do with thee? get thee to the prophets of thy father,
and to the prophets of thy mother.   And the king of
Israel said unto him, Nay : for the LORD hath called

---

9.   and the king of Edom: Edom was in a state of vassalage
to Judah, though, according to 1 Kings xxii. 47 (cf. 2 Kings
viii. 20), there was at this time no Edomite king actually reigning.

11.   Is there not here a prophet of the Lord etc.   It is the
pious king Jehoshaphat who in this critical state of affairs suggests
consultation with one of Jehovah's prophets (cf. *v.* 14).

which poured water on the hands of Elijah: i.e. acted as
Elijah's servant ; cf. 1 Kings xix. 21.   The Oriental custom of
pouring water on the hands of a master (to wash them) is alluded
to.

12.   The word of the Lord is with him: the fact that Elisha
has been the personal attendant of so great a prophet as Elijah
at once legitimizes him in the eyes of Jehoshaphat; contrast
1 Kings xxii.   How Elisha came to be with the army is not
stated ; his appearance may have been due to some mysterious
prophetic impulse.

13.   to the prophets of thy father etc.: i.e. the Baal-prophets;
cf. 1 Kings xviii. 19.

Nay : for the Lord etc.: 'Nay, but it is Jehovah who' etc.
The point of Jehoram's reply is that it is Jehovah who (through

these three kings together to deliver them into the hand
of Moab. And Elisha said, As the LORD of hosts liveth, 14
before whom I stand, surely, were it not that I regard
the presence of Jehoshaphat the king of Judah, I would
not look toward thee, nor see thee. But now bring me 15
a minstrel. And it came to pass, when the minstrel
played, that the hand of the LORD came upon him. And 16
he said, Thus saith the LORD, Make this valley full of
trenches. For thus saith the LORD, Ye shall not see 17
wind, neither shall ye see rain, yet that valley shall be
filled with water: and ye shall drink, both ye and your
cattle and your beasts. And this is but a light thing in 18
the sight of the LORD : he will also deliver the Moabites
into your hand. And ye shall smite every fenced city, 19

His prophets) has sanctioned the expedition. Probably such
prophets as those described in 1 Kings xxii. 5 f. are referred to.

14. before whom I stand: i.e. whom I serve.

15. And it came to pass: rather 'And it used to be'; the
tense is frequentative. The aid of religious music was invoked
in order to arouse the prophetic spirit ; cf. 1 Sam. x. 5 ('a band
of prophets...and a harp before them'). Such stimulus was a
feature of the earlier and cruder manifestations of prophecy, and
had probably been kept up in the prophetic guilds which figure
so largely in the Elisha-narratives. By 'minstrel' a harpist (or
player on some stringed instrument) is meant.

the hand of the Lord: a frequent expression for the trance-
like condition in which the prophetic revelation was received;
cf. Is. viii. 11 ('the Lord spake unto me with a strong hand').

16. Make this valley full of trenches: lit. 'make this wadi
pits pits'; the place meant is probably the *Wadi el-Ahsa* ('valley
of the sandy water-pits'), which marks the natural boundary
between Moab and Edom. Pits were to be dug in the sand, and
water could then be obtained without the aid of rain or wind.
A peculiarity of the region referred to is that the water which
drains down from the mountains is largely retained beneath the
sandy surface by the underlying rocky bed; consequently it can
readily be reached by digging pits in the sand. This course of
action, which was suggested by the prophet, shows an accurate
knowledge of local conditions.

17. your cattle: read with LXX (Luc.) 'your host' (army),
as in *v*. 9.

and every choice city, and shall fell every good tree, and
stop all fountains of water, and mar every good piece of
20 land with stones.   And it came to pass in the morning,
about the time of offering the oblation, that, behold, there
came water by the way of Edom, and the country was
filled with water.

iii. 21–27.   *Moab conquered and ravaged.*

21 Now when all the Moabites heard that the kings were
come up to fight against them, they gathered themselves together, all that were able to put on armour, and
22 upward, and stood on the border.   And they rose up
early in the morning, and the sun shone upon the water,
and the Moabites saw the water over against them as
23 red as blood : and they said, This is blood ; the kings are
surely destroyed, and they have smitten each man his

---

19.   and every choice city: omit with LXX.

20.   about the time of offering the oblation: cf. 1 Kings
xviii. 29, 36.   The daily offering of the morning and evening
oblation was evidently an old-established custom, which prevailed
in the older sanctuaries as well as in the Temple, where it was
perpetuated after the exile.   In later times the morning oblation
was offered as soon as the first streaks of dawn were plainly
visible.

there came water by the way of Edom: rather 'from the way
[direction] of Edom.'   Apparently owing to a sudden rain-storm
in the mountains of Seir a rush of water flowed into the dry wadi,
and overflowing into the pits (which already had water in their
bottoms) filled them up, and also spread partly over the surface
of 'the country.'

21.   Now when all the Moabites heard etc.: rather 'Now all
Moab had heard...and had been summoned together.'   'All that
were able to put on armour (rather a girdle) and upwards' means
all of adult age, able to bear arms.

and stood on the border: i.e. the southern border.

22.   as red as blood: the effect of the red rays of the morning
sun shining on the water.

23.   are surely destroyed: rather (with the margin) 'have
surely fought together.'   The Moabites supposed that the con-
federates had fallen out among themselves—a not unlikely
contingency; cf. Judges vii. 22 ; 2 Chron. xx. 23.

fellow: now therefore, Moab, to the spoil. And when 24
they came to the camp of Israel, the Israelites rose up
and smote the Moabites, so that they fled before them :
and they went forward into the land smiting the Moabites.
And they beat down the cities ; and on every good piece 25
of land they cast every man his stone, and filled it ; and
they stopped all the fountains of water, and felled all the
good trees : until in Kir-hareseth *only* they left the stones
thereof; howbeit the slingers went about it, and smote it.
And when the king of Moab saw that the battle was too 26
sore for him, he took with him seven hundred men that
drew sword, to break through unto the king of Edom :
but they could not. Then he took his eldest son that 27
should have reigned in his stead, and offered him for a

---

24. and they went forward etc.: read, with LXX, 'and
they kept pressing forward, smiting Moab as they went.'

25. And they beat down the cities etc.: the tenses are
frequentative: 'And the cities they would overthrow' etc.
The barbarous methods of warfare here described were universal
in antiquity. By the destruction of palm-groves an enemy's
country has often been made a desert. This particular method
of warfare is forbidden in Deut. xx. 19 f.

until in Kir-hareseth etc.: this part of the text is badly
corrupted. Klostermann (partly following the LXX [Luc.])
has suggested a restoration of the text, which, slightly modified,
reads: 'And they harried Moab until her sons were left in Kir-
hareseth' [and the slingers went about it and smote it]. Kir-
hareseth which is mentioned in Is. xvi. 7, 11 is identical with
the 'Kir of Moab' of Is. xv. 1. It has been identified with the
modern *Kerak*, occupying a position of immense natural strength
on a steep cliff, about twelve miles north of the *Wadi el-Aḥsa*.

26. unto the king of Edom: the attempted sortie was made
in the direction of the Edomite lines—perhaps because they were
the weakest, or possibly because the Edomites were unwilling
allies against Moab.

27. Then he took his eldest son etc.: as a last desperate
expedient Mesha sacrifices his eldest son to Chemosh, the
offended national god of Moab (cf. line 5 of the Moabite stone,
which reads : 'And Chemosh was angry with his land '). Micah
(vi. 7) refers to such human sacrifices ('Shall I give my firstborn
for my transgression?'): cf. also Gen. xxii.

burnt offering upon the wall. And there was great wrath
against Israel: and they departed from him, and returned
to their own land.

IV. 1–VI. 23. STORIES FROM THE LIFE OF ELISHA.

iv. 1–7. *The widow's pot of oil.*

4 Now there cried a certain woman of the wives of the
   sons of the prophets unto Elisha, saying, Thy servant my
   husband is dead: and thou knowest that thy servant did
   fear the LORD: and the creditor is come to take unto
2 him my two children to be bondmen. And Elisha said
   unto her, What shall I do for thee? tell me; what hast
   thou in the house? And she said, Thine handmaid hath
3 not any thing in the house, save a pot of oil. Then he
   said, Go, borrow thee vessels abroad of all thy neighbours,
4 even empty vessels; borrow not a few. And thou shalt
   go in, and shut the door upon thee and upon thy sons,
   and pour out into all those vessels; and thou shalt set
5 aside that which is full. So she went from him, and

And there was great wrath against Israel: i.e. the wrath
of Chemosh, which had been appeased by the sacrifice of the
Moabite king, was now turned against Israel. The sacrifice had
been offered **upon the wall** in the sight of the besiegers, and
doubtless produced a deep impression upon them. It must be
remembered that the Israelites of this period fully believed in
the power of a national god within his own territory (cf. Judges
xi. 24).

they departed from him etc.: the siege had to be raised.

iv. 1–7. With this section 1 Kings xvii. 8–16 should be
compared.

1. of the wives of the sons of the prophets: thus the 'sons
of the prophets,' though living in community, were not celibate.

the creditor is come etc.: the creditor was entitled to take
the children of the debtor as bondservants; cf. Ex. xxi. 7;
Neh. v. 5.

2. oil: i.e. olive oil, which was much used, in a variety of
ways, among the Hebrews.

5. So she went from him: add with LXX (Luc.) 'and did
so.'

shut the door upon her and upon her sons; they brought *the vessels* to her, and she poured out. And it came to 6 pass, when the vessels were full, that she said unto her son, Bring me yet a vessel. And he said unto her, There is not a vessel more. And the oil stayed. Then she 7 came and told the man of God. And he said, Go, sell the oil, and pay thy debt, and live thou and thy sons of the rest.

iv. 8–37.   *The restoration of the Shunammite's son.*

And it fell on a day, that Elisha passed to Shunem, 8 where was a great woman; and she constrained him to eat bread. And so it was, that as oft as he passed by, he turned in thither to eat bread. And she said unto her 9 husband, Behold now, I perceive that this is an holy man of God, which passeth by us continually. Let us make, I 10 pray thee, a little chamber on the wall; and let us set for him there a bed, and a table, and a stool, and a candle-stick: and it shall be, when he cometh to us, that he shall turn in thither. And it fell on a day, that he came thither, 11 and he turned into the chamber and lay there. And he 12 said to Gehazi his servant, Call this Shunammite. And when he had called her, she stood before him. And he 13 said unto him, Say now unto her, Behold, thou hast been careful for us with all this care; what is to be done for

---

8–37. Cf. with this narrative 1 Kings xvii. 17–24. This story also illustrates how proper reverence for the man of God could be rewarded.

8.   Shunem: the modern *Sōlem* in the plain of Jezreel, situated on the south-west slope of a hill, overlooking the plain which is now known as *Nebi Dāhī*.

as oft as he passed by: on his frequent journeys between Gilgal and Carmel (cf. iii. 1, iv. 38, 25) he would pass over the plain of Jezreel.

10.   a little chamber on the wall: read, with the margin, 'a little chamber with walls': i.e. a permanent structure, and not a mere temporary erection of branches etc. or a tent on the roof (cf. 2 Sam. xvi. 20; Neh. viii. 16).

thee? wouldest thou be spoken for to the king, or to the
captain of the host? And she answered, I dwell among
14 mine own people. And he said, What then is to be done
for her? And Gehazi answered, Verily she hath no son,
15 and her husband is old. And he said, Call her. And
16 when he had called her, she stood in the door. And he
said, At this season, when the time cometh round, thou
shalt embrace a son. And she said, Nay, my lord, thou
17 man of God, do not lie unto thine handmaid. And the
woman conceived, and bare a son at that season, when
18 the time came round, as Elisha had said unto her. And
when the child was grown, it fell on a day, that he went
19 out to his father to the reapers. And he said unto his
father, My head, my head. And he said to his servant,
20 Carry him to his mother. And when he had taken him,
and brought him to his mother, he sat on her knees till
21 noon, and then died. And she went up, and laid him on

---

13. to the king: not necessarily Jehoram; the king intended
may not improbably have been Jehu whom Elisha had sent a
prophet to anoint.

the captain of the host: i.e. the commander-in-chief, the
most powerful personage next to the king.

I dwell among mine own people: the great lady had no need
or inclination to seek favour from the king; she was contented
to dwell with her own people, who could no doubt provide her
with sufficient occupation, and would be well able to sustain
their rights.

14. she hath no son: childlessness was at once a misfortune
and a reproach; cf. Gen. xxx. 23; 1 Sam. i. 6, 7 etc.

16. At this season, when the time cometh round: this phrase
is found again only in Gen. xviii. 10, 14. It probably means
'at the reviving time,' i.e. next spring, the season of the year
when life revives.

do not lie: i.e. 'raise no delusive hopes': cf. Gen. xviii. 12,
13.

19. My head, my head: the child had a sunstroke, the time
of year being the hot season of harvest; cf. Judith viii. 3 ('he
stood over them that bound sheaves in the field, and the heat
came upon his head, and he took to his bed and died').

21. and laid him on the bed etc.: cf. 1 Kings xvii. 19.

the bed of the man of God, and shut *the door* upon him, and went out. And she called unto her husband, and 22 said, Send me, I pray thee, one of the servants, and one of the asses, that I may run to the man of God, and come again. And he said, Wherefore wilt thou go to him 23 to-day? it is neither new moon nor sabbath. And she · said, It shall be well. Then she saddled an ass, and 24 said to her servant, Drive, and go forward; slacken me not the riding, except I bid thee. So she went, and 25 came unto the man of God to mount Carmel. And it came to pass, when the man of God saw her afar off, that he said to Gehazi his servant, Behold, yonder is the Shunammite: run, I pray thee, now to meet her, and say 26 unto her, Is it well with thee? is it well with thy husband? is it well with the child? And she answered, It is well. And when she came to the man of God to the hill, she 27 caught hold of his feet. And Gehazi came near to thrust her away; but the man of God said, Let her alone: for her soul is vexed within her; and the LORD hath hid it from me, and hath not told me. Then she said, Did 28 I desire a son of my lord? did I not say, Do not deceive me? Then he said to Gehazi, Gird up thy loins, and 29

---

23. **new moon nor sabbath**: on these holy days it was, apparently, customary to pay visits to prophets or sanctuaries. A reference to 'new moons' and 'sabbaths' occurs in Amos viii. 5. Such journeys might involve comparatively long distances (in this case about twenty-five miles).

It shall be well: the meaning is rather equivalent to 'it is all right.'

25. **to mount Carmel**: Carmel was one of the centres of prophetic activity (cf. 1 Kings xviii. 31 f.), and Elisha was frequently there (cf. *v.* 9 above).

26. **Is it well** etc.: her coming at such a time would be unusual, and would naturally excite surprise. The Shunammite's answer is a simple affirmative; she would lay bare her grief only to the man of God himself.

28. **Did I desire** etc.: instead of stating her complaint directly, she uses the language of reproach; cf. 1 Kings xvii. 18.

take my staff in thine hand, and go thy way: if thou
meet any man, salute him not; and if any salute thee,
answer him not again: and lay my staff upon the face of
30 the child.   And the mother of the child said, As the
LORD liveth, and as thy soul liveth, I will not leave thee.
31 And he arose, and followed her.   And Gehazi passed on
before them, and laid the staff upon the face of the child;
but there was neither voice, nor hearing.   Wherefore he
returned to meet him, and told him, saying, The child is
32 not awaked.   And when Elisha was come into the house,
33 behold, the child was dead, and laid upon his bed.   He
went in therefore, and shut the door upon them twain,
34 and prayed unto the LORD.   And he went up, and lay
upon the child, and put his mouth upon his mouth,
and his eyes upon his eyes, and his hands upon his
hands: and he stretched himself upon him; and the
35 flesh of the child waxed warm.   Then he returned, and
walked in the house once to and fro; and went up, and
stretched himself upon him: and the child sneezed seven

---

29.   salute him not: cf. Luke x. 4.   The injunction in each
case was given in order that time should not be lost in exchanging
tedious salutations, such as are common in the East.

lay my staff etc.: the prophet seems to have thought at first
that the child might not be really dead.   For the belief that
contact with objects, closely associated with men of special
powers, might be the medium for imparting power or virtue
cf. Acts xix. 12 ('unto the sick were carried away from his body
handkerchiefs or aprons, and the diseases departed from them').
Here the prophet's staff is apparently thought of in a similar
way.

30.   I will not leave thee: the mother felt that the prophet's
personal presence was essential.

31.   neither voice, nor hearing: cf. 1 Kings xviii. 26, 29;
there was no sign of life.

33.   He went in etc.: cf. 1 Kings xvii. 17-24, esp. *v*. 19.

34.   stretched himself upon him: lit. 'crouched over him.'

35.   he returned: *sc*. from the bed.

walked...to and fro: an indication of intense excitement.

the child sneezed etc.: the repeated sneezing showed that
the child was beginning to breathe again.   The LXX (B),

times, and the child opened his eyes. And he called 36
Gehazi, and said, Call this Shunammite. So he called
her. And when she was come in unto him, he said, Take
up thy son. Then she went in, and fell at his feet, and 37
bowed herself to the ground; and she took up her son,
and went out.

iv. 38-41. *Death in the pot.*

And Elisha came again to Gilgal: and there was 38
a dearth in the land; and the sons of the prophets were
sitting before him: and he said unto his servant, Set on
the great pot, and seethe pottage for the sons of the
prophets. And one went out into the field to gather 39
herbs, and found a wild vine, and gathered thereof wild
gourds his lap full, and came and shred them into the pot
of pottage: for they knew them not. So they poured out 40
for the men to eat. And it came to pass, as they were
eating of the pottage, that they cried out, and said, O
man of God, there is death in the pot. And they could

---

however, omits this sentence; the text then reads: 'and he
stretched himself upon the child until seven times.'

38. came again to Gilgal: or 'had returned to Gilgal,'
probably on a visit. The community of the prophets at Gilgal
apparently led a common life, living together in one place (cf.
vi. 1), and having meals together. Elisha had his own private
house (probably in Samaria; cf. v. 9).

a dearth, or **the dearth**: i.e. the seven years' famine foretold
in viii. 1.

were sitting before him: as disciples before a master.

seethe pottage: cf. Gen. xxv. 29.

39. a wild vine...wild gourds: wild gourds or cucumbers,
which were mistaken for edible gourds, may be meant. These
are bitter in taste, and, if eaten, have a violent purgative effect.
The Vulgate understands the colocynth to be meant, a plant of
the same family, and producing similar effects.

40. So they poured out: LXX has the singular, 'so he
poured out,' i.e. the servant (cf. *vv.* 38 and 41), who, according
to the LXX, was Gehazi.

there is death in the pot: the bitter taste made them think
of poison.

41 not eat thereof. But he said, Then bring meal. And
he cast it into the pot; and he said, Pour out for the
people, that they may eat. And there was no harm in
the pot.

iv. 42-44. *A hundred prophets miraculously fed.*

42 And there came a man from Baal-shalishah, and
brought the man of God bread of the firstfruits, twenty
loaves of barley, and fresh ears of corn in his sack. And
43 he said, Give unto the people, that they may eat. And
his servant said, What, should I set this before an
hundred men? But he said, Give the people, that they
may eat; for thus saith the LORD, They shall eat, and
44 shall leave thereof. So he set it before them, and they
did eat, and left thereof, according to the word of the
LORD.

v. 1-19. *Elisha heals Naaman.*

5   Now Naaman, captain of the host of the king of Syria,
was a great man with his master, and honourable, because
by him the LORD had given victory unto Syria: he was

---

42. Baal-shalishah: the place has been identified by Conder
with a ruined site *Khirbet Kefr Thilth* about fourteen miles
north-west of *Jiljilie.*

bread of the firstfruits: according to the Law (cf. Numb.
xviii. 13; Deut. xviii. 4) the firstfruits of grain were to be offered
to the priest. The custom of giving such to a prophet is not
elsewhere referred to.

fresh ears etc.: or, better, perhaps, 'freshly plucked garden
growth (Heb. *karmel*) in his wallet'; cf. Lev. ii. 14, xxiii. 14.

43. before an hundred men: i.e. of the 'sons of the prophets':
the narrative is closely connected with the preceding section, and
clearly implies the same situation. The incident took place during
the great famine. That the community of the prophets at Gilgal
was large may be inferred from vi. 1.

v. 1. honourable: lit. 'lifted up of face,' i.e. respected; cf.
Is. iii. 3.

by him etc.: it is noticeable that the victories won by Naaman
are ascribed not to Hadad or Rimmon, but to Jehovah, in accordance with the high prophetic view.

also a mighty man of valour, *but he was* a leper. And 2
the Syrians had gone out in bands, and had brought
away captive out of the land of Israel a little maid; and
she waited on Naaman's wife. And she said unto her 3
mistress, Would God my lord were with the prophet that
is in Samaria! then would he recover him of his leprosy.
And one went in, and told his lord, saying, Thus and thus 4
said the maid that is of the land of Israel. And the king 5
of Syria said, Go to, go, and I will send a letter unto the
king of Israel. And he departed, and took with him ten
talents of silver, and six thousand *pieces* of gold, and ten
changes of raiment. And he brought the letter to the 6
king of Israel, saying, And now when this letter is come
unto thee, behold, I have sent Naaman my servant to
thee, that thou mayest recover him of his leprosy. And 7

---

a mighty man of valour: these words, which are probably
a gloss on 'great man' above, are omitted by the LXX (Luc.):
read 'but the man was a leper.'

2. in bands: i.e. in marauding bands. Such raids were
apparently made during a time when the countries were not
formally at war, and this fact will explain how it was that a
Jewish girl had been made a captive at such a time.

3. in Samaria: Samaria throughout this narrative is obviously
regarded as the prophet's place of residence; here, according to
v. 9, he had a private house.

4. And one went in etc.: the LXX (Luc.) reads: 'And she
[i.e. Naaman's wife] went in and told her lord, and he told the
king, and said: Thus and thus' etc. This is probably the right
text.

5. with him: lit. 'in his hand.'

ten talents of silver...gold: the money talent was equal to
sixty minas, and the mina to fifty shekels; thus ten silver talents
would be equivalent to thirty thousand shekels. A gold piece
would be a gold shekel (worth about forty-five shillings of our
money). The total sum is very large.

changes of raiment: cf. Gen. xlv. 22; Judges xiv. 12, 13, 19.

6. And now etc.: only the last (important) part of the letter
is cited; the introductory part containing the conventional forms
of greeting is naturally omitted.

that thou mayest recover: the tone is peremptory—the king
of Israel is addressed as a vassal.

it came to pass, when the king of Israel had read the
letter, that he rent his clothes, and said, Am I God, to
kill and to make alive, that this man doth send unto me
to recover a man of his leprosy? but consider, I pray you,
8 and see how he seeketh a quarrel against me.   And it
was so, when Elisha the man of God heard that the king
of Israel had rent his clothes, that he sent to the king,
saying, Wherefore hast thou rent thy clothes? let him
come now to me, and he shall know that there is a
9 prophet in Israel.   So Naaman came with his horses
and with his chariots, and stood at the door of the house
10 of Elisha.   And Elisha sent a messenger unto him,
saying, Go and wash in Jordan seven times, and thy flesh
11 shall come again to thee, and thou shalt be clean.   But
Naaman was wroth, and went away, and said, Behold,
I thought, He will surely come out to me, and stand, and
call on the name of the LORD his God, and wave his
12 hand over the place, and recover the leper.   Are not
Abanah and Pharpar, the rivers of Damascus, better than

---

7. Am I God etc.: cf. 1 Sam. ii. 6 ('The Lord killeth and
maketh alive').

he seeketh a quarrel: or 'opportunity or pretext for renewing
war'; the corresponding noun, rendered 'occasion,' occurs in
Judges xiv. 4 ('he sought an occasion against the Philistines').
For a similar sentiment cf. 1 Kings xx. 7.

8. there is a prophet etc.: the fame of the prophet, which
has reached Damascus, shall be justified by the event.

10. sent a messenger: the prophet does not appear in
person, but communicates with the great man through a servant
(cf. iv. 12 f. in the similar case of the Shunammite).

11. Naaman was wroth etc.: he resented the indignity.

12. Are not Abanah and Pharpar etc.: the wholesome
streams of Damascus are as good for such a purpose as the
waters of Jordan.   The **Abanah** (pronounced by the Masoretes
Amana, and so some other authorities) is identified with the
present *Nahr Barada* (the classical Chrysorrhoas), which waters
the plain of Damascus, rising in the Anti-Lebanon, and flowing
eastward in seven streams.   The **Pharpar** may be identified with
the *A'waj*, which, rising in the great Hermon, flows by Damascus

all the waters of Israel? may I not wash in them, and be
clean? So he turned and went away in a rage. And his 13
servants came near, and spake unto him, and said, My
father, if the prophet had bid thee do some great thing,
wouldest thou not have done it? how much rather then,
when he saith to thee, Wash, and be clean? Then went 14
he down, and dipped *himself* seven times in Jordan,
according to the saying of the man of God: and his flesh
came again like unto the flesh of a little child, and he
was clean. And he returned to the man of God, he and 15
all his company, and came, and stood before him: and
he said, Behold now, I know that there is no God in all
the earth, but in Israel: now therefore, I pray thee, take
a present of thy servant. But he said, As the LORD 16
liveth, before whom I stand, I will receive none. And he
urged him to take it; but he refused. And Naaman 17
said, If not, yet I pray thee let there be given to thy
servant two mules' burden of earth; for thy servant will

---

in the south (the name 'Pharpar' may be preserved in that of
the *Wadi Barbar*, whose waters do not, however, now flow into
the *A'waj*). Both are mountain streams, with clear cool water,
in this respect contrasting with the turbid Jordan.

13. My father: probably this is a corruption of the Heb.
word meaning 'if,' which is required, but is not expressed, in
the present Heb. text. Such a form of address to a master by
servants is not usual.

14. Then went he down: *sc.* from Samaria to the bed of the
Jordan.

seven times: the number denotes completeness.

15. there is no God...but in Israel: Naaman like his con-
temporaries (Israelite and other) had the territorial conception
of gods who were potent in particular localities. Even now,
when he recognizes the unique power of Israel's God, he still
conceives of this God as primarily in the land of Israel. At the
same time such a confession of one only living God is surprising
in the mouth of a heathen in the ninth century B.C. Cf. Is. xlv.
14.

present: lit. 'blessing'; cf. 1 Sam. xxx. 26.

17. two mules' burden of earth: he still conceives of the
God of Israel as a land-God, who could only be worshipped on

henceforth offer neither burnt offering nor sacrifice unto
18 other gods, but unto the LORD.   In this thing the LORD
pardon thy servant; when my master goeth into the
house of Rimmon to worship there, and he leaneth on
my hand, and I bow myself in the house of Rimmon,
when I bow myself in the house of Rimmon, the LORD
19 pardon thy servant in this thing.   And he said unto him,
Go in peace.   So he departed from him a little way.

v. 20–27.   *The punishment of Gehazi.*

20   But Gehazi, the servant of Elisha the man of God,
said, Behold, my master hath spared this Naaman the
Syrian, in not receiving at his hands that which he
brought: as the LORD liveth, I will run after him, and
21 take somewhat of him.   So Gehazi followed after Naaman.
And when Naaman saw one running after him, he lighted
down from the chariot to meet him, and said, Is all well?

His own soil; hence some Israelitish soil must be taken with him
back to Damascus.   Such ideas were universal at the time.   For
altars of earth cf. Ex. xx. 24.

18.   Rimmon: the Assyrian *Rammânu,* a thunder-god
(*ramâmu* in Assyrian = 'to thunder').   Rimmon was identified
by the Assyrians with the Aramean Hadad (cf. the name Hadad-
rimmon in Zech. xii. 11).

to worship: or 'bow myself,' as the same Hebrew word is
rendered further on in the same verse.   The worship referred to
would be the perfunctory homage rendered to the official god of
the state.   Though he had solemnly promised to serve no other
god but Jehovah, Naaman asks to be excused for participating in
this way in a state function.   The prophet's 'Go in peace' is a
formula of assent to this request.

19.   a little way: lit. 'a *kibrath* of land' (cf. Gen. xxxv. 16,
xlviii. 7).   The exact meaning is uncertain; it probably denotes
a short, undetermined, distance.

20.   this Naaman the Syrian: rather 'this Syrian Naaman';
his thought is, 'it is foolish not to despoil this foreigner.'

21.   one: read 'him.'

he lighted down etc.: lit. 'fell,' i.e. got down from his chariot
hastily—a mark of respect.   Such honour is due to the prophet
through his servant.

And he said, All is well. My master hath sent me, saying, 22
Behold, even now there be come to me from the hill
country of Ephraim two young men of the sons of the
prophets ; give them, I pray thee, a talent of silver, and
two changes of raiment. And Naaman said, Be content, 23
take two talents. And he urged him, and bound two
talents of silver in two bags, with two changes of raiment,
and laid them upon two of his servants ; and they bare
them before him. And when he came to the hill, he 24
took them from their hand, and bestowed them in the
house : and he let the men go, and they departed. But 25
he went in, and stood before his master. And Elisha
said unto him, Whence comest thou, Gehazi ? And he
said, Thy servant went no whither. And he said unto 26
him, Went not mine heart *with thee*, when the man
turned again from his chariot to meet thee ? Is it a time
to receive money, and to receive garments, and oliveyards

---

23. upon two of his servants: i.e. of Naaman's servants
('young men'). Others take it to mean 'his (Gehazi's) two
servants,' supposing that Gehazi had taken two young men with
him. This is less natural.

24. the hill: Heb. '*Ophel*. This term is usually supposed
to mean, as the R.V. interprets it, 'the hill' (lit. 'the swelling,'
'mound'); elsewhere it has reference to the south spur of the
eastern hill in Jerusalem (i.e. the site of the ancient city of David) ;
here, presumably, it means some hill in Samaria (the term also
occurs in Mesha's inscription, line 21 f.). Burney, however, has
given good reasons for interpreting the term in the sense of
'citadel' (keep, possibly 'a bulging or rounded keep'). In this
case what is meant here is that Elisha's residence was within the
citadel of Samaria (the narrative implies that he was on good
terms with the king); and when Gehazi came to the gate of the
citadel, he took the bags from the servants, 'and bestowed them
in the house' (i.e. laid them up carefully in the prophet's house).

25. went in: *sc.* into the chamber of his master.

26. Is it a time etc.: the text, as translated, means: the
present is no time for amassing wealth; it is a time of famine
and national distress. The LXX, however, with one small change,
reads: 'And now thou hast taken the money, and wilt take
garments...maidservants, and the leprosy of Naaman shall cleave'
etc. Among the gifts he has deceitfully taken is the giver's leprosy.

and vineyards, and sheep and oxen, and menservants and
27 maidservants? The leprosy therefore of Naaman shall
cleave unto thee, and unto thy seed for ever. And he
went out from his presence a leper *as white* as snow.

vi. 1-7. *Elisha makes the axe-head swim.*

6   And the sons of the prophets said unto Elisha, Behold
now, the place where we dwell before thee is too strait
2 for us. Let us go, we pray thee, unto Jordan, and take
thence every man a beam, and let us make us a place
there, where we may dwell. And he answered, Go ye.
3 And one said, Be content, I pray thee, and go with thy
4 servants. And he answered, I will go. So he went with
them. And when they came to Jordan, they cut down
5 wood. But as one was felling a beam, the axe-head fell
into the water: and he cried, and said, Alas, my master!
6 for it was borrowed. And the man of God said, Where
fell it? And he shewed him the place. And he cut down

---

vi. 1-7. The following narrative continues those in ch. iv.
38-41 and 42-44, and implies a similar situation. 'The place,'
apparently, is Gilgal, where the prophetic community lives a
common life. Chapter v. has probably been inserted from
another source.

1.   dwell before thee : this certainly seems to imply that at
the period of the narrative Elisha was living with the prophetic
community; contrast chapter **v.**, which probably refers to a
different period in the prophet's life, where he is represented as
living in his own private house in Samaria.

2.   Let us go...unto Jordan : the Jordan valley is chosen
as the site of the new settlement, perhaps because the materials
for building 'dwellings' were more abundant there.

4.   wood : Heb. 'the timber,' i.e. the timber required.

5.   felling a beam : the proper object of 'fell' would, of
course, be ' tree,' not 'beam '; by a slight change the text would
read 'swinging the axe.'

6.   a stick etc. : the stick was thrown into the water where
the iron axe-head had sunk, and (? by contact with it) is made
to impart to the iron, in a mysterious and supernatural manner,
its own power of floating.

a stick, and cast it in thither, and made the iron to swim.
And he said, Take it up to thee. So he put out his hand, **7**
and took it.

vi. 8–23. *A Syrian force entrapped by Elisha.*

Now the king of Syria warred against Israel ; and he **8**
took counsel with his servants, saying, In such and such
a place shall be my camp. And the man of God sent **9**
unto the king of Israel, saying, Beware that thou pass
not such a place; for thither the Syrians are coming
down. And the king of Israel sent to the place which **10**
the man of God told him and warned him of; and he
saved himself there, not once nor twice. And the heart **11**
of the king of Syria was sore troubled for this thing ; and
he called his servants, and said unto them, Will ye not
shew me which of us is for the king of Israel? And one **12**
of his servants said, Nay, my lord, O king: but Elisha,
the prophet that is in Israel, telleth the king of Israel the
words that thou speakest in thy bedchamber. And he **13**
said, Go and see where he is, that I may send and fetch
him. And it was told him, saying, Behold, he is in
Dothan. Therefore sent he thither horses, and chariots, **14**

---

8. the king of Syria warred etc. : a state of war between
Syria and Israel exists (contrast ch. v.), though hostilities are
apparently confined to marauding expeditions. The names of
the kings in whose reigns these events took place are not given.

shall be my camp : the text is probably corrupt ; read
'conceal yourselves.'

9. are coming down : read (by a slight textual change) ' are
concealed.'

10. sent : i.e. sent an adequate force to repel the raid.

saved himself : rather ' was wary,' ' on his guard,' i.e. saved
himself from surprise (the same Hebrew word is used as in *v.* 9
for 'beware').

11. which of us is for etc. : read, following LXX, 'who
betrayeth us to.'

13. Dothan (contracted form of *Dothain*, LXX *Dothaim*) :
it lay about ten miles north-east of Samaria, and is identified
with the modern *Tell Dōthān*, a site covered with ruins. It

and a great host : and they came by night, and com-
15 passed the city about. And when the servant of the
man of God was risen early, and gone forth, behold, an
host with horses and chariots was round about the city.
And his servant said unto him, Alas, my master! how
16 shall we do? And he answered, Fear not: for they that
17 be with us are more than they that be with them. And
Elisha prayed, and said, LORD, I pray thee, open his
eyes, that he may see. And the LORD opened the eyes
of the young man; and he saw: and, behold, the mountain
was full of horses and chariots of fire round about Elisha.
18 And when they came down to him, Elisha prayed unto
the LORD, and said, Smite this people, I pray thee, with
blindness. And he smote them with blindness according
19 to the word of Elisha. And Elisha said unto them, This
is not the way, neither is this the city: follow me, and

---

gave its name to a narrow pass, on level ground, through which
crossed the caravan-road (traversing the plain of Jezreel) from
Gilead to Egypt ; cf. Gen. xxxvii. 17.

15. And when the servant etc. : the text is in some confusion here : read, following LXX (Luc.), 'and he [Elisha]
arose early on the morrow in the morning and went out and
behold ' etc.

16. they that be with us etc. : cf. 2 Chron. xxxii. 7, 8.

17. And the Lord opened the eyes etc. : cf. ii. 10, 12 ;
' young man ' should be 'servant ' as in *v.* 15.

the mountain : Dothan lay on a hill in the midst of a narrow
plain ; ' the mountain ' thus suits well the elevated ground on
which the place stood.

horses and chariots of fire : cf. ii. 17 and notes.

18. when they came down : i.e. from the mountains which
surrounded the little plain, where the enemy had encamped
during the night. The Syriac, however, reads : 'And they [i.e.
Elisha and his servant] went down to them '—i.e. inspired with
courage by the vision of the heavenly host around them they
descended from the hill on which Dothan lay to the valley below
to meet the Syrians (so Ball).

blindness : the Hebrew term used is a peculiar one, and
occurs again only in Gen. xix. 11 ; it denotes not exactly
blindness, but 'a dazing effect accompanied by mental bewilder-
ment and confusion ' (Ball).

I will bring you to the man whom ye seek. And he led
them to Samaria.   And it came to pass, when they were 20
come into Samaria, that Elisha said, LORD, open the
eyes of these men, that they may see.   And the LORD
opened their eyes, and they saw ; and, behold, they were
in the midst of Samaria.   And the king of Israel said 21
unto Elisha, when he saw them, My father, shall I smite
them? shall I smite them?   And he answered, Thou 22
shalt not smite them: wouldest thou smite those whom
thou hast taken captive with thy sword and with thy
bow? set bread and water before them, that they may
eat and drink, and go to their master.   And he prepared 23
great provision for them: and when they had eaten and
drunk, he sent them away, and they went to their master.
And the bands of Syria came no more into the land of
Israel.

---

21. My father: cf. xiii. 14 (also ii. 12, viii. 9).   The king
and the prophet are evidently on friendly terms (cf. ch. v.).
      shall I...shall I etc.: the repetition reflects the king's
eagerness.
      22. thou hast taken captive etc.: read with LXX (Luc.)
'whom thou hast not taken captive' etc.   It was certainly not
unusual in old Israel (cf. 1 Sam. xv. 3, 33) to slay prisoners of
war who fell under the ban. though this usage was mitigated in
later times.   Here the king's first impulse was to have the
prisoners massacred—an impulse checked by the prophet.
      23. And the bands etc.: impressed by the prophet's power,
and probably awe-struck, the Syrians abandoned their raids.
      24–31. This section (vi. 24–vii. 20) resembles in general
character iii. 4 f.   Here, as there, though Elisha is the central
figure, there is a strong political background, and a general
resemblance to the popular historical narrative to which 1 Kings
xx. and xxii. belong.   Possibly the present narrative has been
derived by the compiler not directly from the Elisha biographical cycle, but from a historical source, similar in general
character to 1 Kings xx. and xxii.   In any case it owes its
present position to the fact that it illustrates the life of the
prophet.
      Apparently the Syrians took advantage of the great famine
referred to in viii. 1 (which lasted seven years) to lay siege to
Samaria.   The chapter illustrates the terrible plight to which
the inhabitants had been reduced by the famine.

VI. 24-VII. 20. THE SIEGE OF SAMARIA AND THE
FAMINE.

vi. 24-31.   *The king's threat.*

24   And it came to pass after this, that Ben-hadad king of
Syria gathered all his host, and went up, and besieged
25 Samaria.   And there was a great famine in Samaria :
and, behold, they besieged it, until an ass's head was
sold for fourscore *pieces* of silver, and the fourth part of
26 a kab of dove's dung for five *pieces* of silver.   And as the
king of Israel was passing by upon the wall, there cried
27 a woman unto him, saying, Help, my lord, O king.   And

---

24. And it came to pass etc.: cf. for the phraseology
1 Kings xx. 1, 2.

after this: probably the chapter originally stood (in the
source) in a different connexion from the present one ; it contradicts *v.* 23.

Ben-hadad: this monarch is not necessarily identical with
the Ben-hadad of 1 Kings xx. 1 (the contemporary of Ahab) ;
not improbably he is the same as the 'Ben-hadad the son of
Hazael,' who, according to 2 Kings xiii. 3, was constantly at
war with Israel during the reign of Jehoahaz, the son of Jehu.

25. an ass's head etc.: ass's flesh would not, in ordinary
circumstances, be eaten at all ; now the head—the cheapest part
—sells at a fabulous price, eighty silver shekels (LXX fifty) :
80 shekels = about £11, reckoning the silver shekel as = 2s. 9d.

a kab of dove's dung : the **kab** is the name of a measure
equivalent to one-eighteenth part of an ephah ; a fourth of a kab
would be rather less than a pint.   The kab is not mentioned
again in the Old Testament, but is well known in later
(Rabbinical) Jewish literature.   **Dove's dung** is the literal
rendering of the Hebrew text as it stands.   As some kind of
possible food is obviously demanded by the context, it has been
supposed that it is a popular name for some vegetable product
(roasted chick peas) ; 'sparrows' dung' is applied in Arabic to
a herb, according to Bochart.   A slight emendation (proposed
by Cheyne) yields the sense 'carob pods,' a poor substitute for
bread.   This may be right.

26. the wall : i.e. the broad rampart of the city wall ; the
king would naturally inspect the defences and encourage the
garrison from time to time by means of this.

he said, If the LORD do not help thee, whence shall
I help thee? out of the threshing-floor, or out of the
winepress? And the king said unto her, What aileth 28
thee? And she answered, This woman said unto me,
Give thy son, that we may eat him to-day, and we will
eat my son to-morrow. So we boiled my son, and did 29
eat him: and I said unto her on the next day, Give thy
son, that we may eat him: and she hath hid her son.
And it came to pass, when the king heard the words of 30
the woman, that he rent his clothes; (now he was passing
by upon the wall;) and the people looked, and, behold,
he had sackcloth within upon his flesh. Then he said, 31
God do so to me, and more also, if the head of Elisha the
son of Shaphat shall stand on him this day.

---

27. If the Lord do not help thee etc.: the Hebrew is
difficult, and the marginal rendering is, perhaps, to be preferred,
'Nay, let the Lord [i.e. Jehovah] help thee.' Note the bitter
irony of the following sentence: 'out of the threshing-floor or
out of the winepress?' The stores of corn and wine—the
regular supplies—had long since been exhausted.

28. And the king said etc.: this sentence logically follows
on *v.* 26.

Give thy son etc.: the suggestion was the neighbour's, who,
however, refuses to carry out her part of the compact, and con-
ceals her son.

30. he rent his clothes: horror-struck at the woman's tale,
which may be illustrated by what has occurred in other sieges;
cf. Lam. iv. 10 ('women have sodden their own children') of
Nebuchadnezzar's siege of Jerusalem. For **passing by** read
with LXX (Luc.) **standing** (upon the wall).

sackcloth within: the rending of the outer garments—which
was itself the outward sign of grief—revealed the fact that the
king had been wearing in secret—next his body—the ascetic
garb of penitence and grief; cf. 1 Kings xxi. 27.

31. God do so to me etc.: the climax of horror had been
reached when women devoured their own children, and now the
king's fury is turned against Elisha, who, for some reason, is
regarded as responsible for what has happened. Probably the
prophet had been holding out promises of divine help to the
besieged, which seemed now to be utterly delusive (cf. *v.* 33).
The king's solicitude for his people is obviously sincere, and evidently appealed to the sympathies of the writer of the narrative.

vi. 32–vii. 2. Elisha predicts speedy relief from famine.

32 But Elisha sat in his house, and the elders sat with
him ; and *the king* sent a man from before him : but ere
the messenger came to him, he said to the elders, See
ye how this son of a murderer hath sent to take away
mine head ? look, when the messenger cometh, shut the
door, and hold the door fast against him : is not the
33 sound of his master's feet behind him ? And while he
yet talked with them, behold, the messenger came down
unto him : and he said, Behold, this evil is of the LORD ;
7 why should I wait for the LORD any longer? And Elisha

---

32. the elders etc.: the 'elders' would be the principal
men of the city, who filled responsible offices in its administration (cf. 1 Kings xxi. 11). These were now assembled
in the prophet's house, having come to consult through him the
will of Jehovah; cf. Ezek. viii. 1, xx. 1. The situation described
shows how important a position the prophet occupied in the
critical state of affairs that had arisen. In a similar manner the
prophet Jeremiah was consulted by Zedekiah and his nobles
during the siege of Jerusalem (cf. Jer. xxi. 1, 2, xxxviii. 14 f.).

32 b, 33. and the king sent a man etc.: as the text at present stands there is evidently some confusion. The words
Behold, this evil is of the Lord (*v.* 33) must be those of the king.
Either all that refers to the messenger must be regarded as a
later addition (so Wellhausen), or some sentences describing
the sending of the messenger and his return, followed by the
coming of the king in person, have fallen out.

32. this son of a murderer : the expression means no
more than 'murderer,' and has reference to the king's present
intention to order the prophet's immediate execution (cf. 'sons
of the prophets' = prophets).

33. behold, the messenger came down : read 'the king'
for 'the messenger' (the two words are very similar in Hebrew),
and so also in *v.* 32 *b*. [The text of 32 *b* and 33, freed from later
additions, and thus slightly emended, will now read as follows :
'And before the king came to him, he said to the elders, See ye
that this son of a murderer hath sent to take away mine head ?
And while he was yet speaking with them, the king came down
unto him, and said, Behold this evil etc.']

why should I wait etc.: apparently the king's murderous
impulse died away in the presence of the prophet ; he is over-
awed, and merely gives expression to his feeling of despair.

said, Hear ye the word of the LORD: thus saith the
LORD, To-morrow about this time shall a measure of fine
flour be *sold* for a shekel, and two measures of barley for
a shekel, in the gate of Samaria.   Then the captain on 2
whose hand the king leaned answered the man of God,
and said, Behold, if the LORD should make windows in
heaven, might this thing be?   And he said, Behold, thou
shalt see it with thine eyes, but shalt not eat thereof.

vii. 3-20.   *Elisha's prophecy brilliantly fulfilled.*

Now there were four leprous men at the entering in of 3
the gate: and they said one to another, Why sit we
here until we die?   If we say, We will enter into the city, 4
then the famine is in the city, and we shall die there:
and if we sit still here, we die also.   Now therefore come,
and let us fall unto the host of the Syrians: if they save
us alive, we shall live; and if they kill us, we shall but
die.   And they rose up in the twilight, to go unto the 5
camp of the Syrians: and when they were come to the
outermost part of the camp of the Syrians, behold, there

---

vii. 1.   a measure : marg. 'seah,' the third part of an ephah.
It was the usual corn measure, and equivalent to about a peck
and a half.

a shekel : this price would still be high.

in the gate : i.e. in the open space within the city-gate which
usually served as market-place.

2.   the captain etc.: or rather 'adjutant' (Heb. *shālîsh*); here
the king's personal attendant is meant, cf. 2 Kings ix. 25 (Bidkar
Jehu's adjutant).   Naaman occupied a similar position in relation
to the king of Syria (cf. v. 18).

windows in heaven: cf. Gen. vii. 11, viii. 2; Mal. iii. 10.
Notice the scoffing tone of the adjutant's remark.

3.   at the entering in of the gate : i.e. at the entrance of the
gate outside the city walls; as unclean they would not be per-
mitted to reside in the city; cf. Lev. xiii. 46 ('without the
camp'); Num. v. 2, 3.

4.   fall unto : i.e. 'desert to' (the regular expression in
Hebrew).

5.   in the twilight : when they would be unobserved from
the city walls.

6 was no man there. For the Lord had made the host of
the Syrians to hear a noise of chariots, and a noise of
horses, even the noise of a great host : and they said one
to another, Lo, the king of Israel hath hired against us
the kings of the Hittites, and the kings of the Egyptians,
7 to come upon us. Wherefore they arose and fled in the
twilight, and left their tents, and their horses, and their
asses, even the camp as it was, and fled for their life.
8 And when these lepers came to the outermost part of the
camp, they went into one tent, and did eat and drink, and
carried thence silver, and gold, and raiment, and went and
hid it ; and they came back, and entered into another tent,
9 and carried thence also, and went and hid it. Then they
said one to another, We do not well : this day is a day of
good tidings, and we hold our peace : if we tarry till the
morning light, punishment will overtake us : now therefore
10 come, let us go and tell the king's household. So they
came and called unto the porter of the city : and they

6. the kings of the Hittites etc. : the cradle of the Hittite
race and the centre of its power lay in Northern Syria between
the Euphrates and Orontes. But it is highly improbable that a
combination of Hittites (in the north) with Egyptians (in the
south) for the relief of Samaria should have been thought of.
Consequently some scholars have explained the mention of
Egypt here as due to confusion, in the mind of the narrator, of
Egypt with Assyria. A more probable hypothesis is here (as
elsewhere in the Hebrew text of the Old Testament) that the
name of Egypt (Heb. *Miṣraim*) has been confused with that of
Muṣri. As the Assyrian inscriptions show, there was a northern
Muṣri (probably referred to also in 1 Kings x. 28), corresponding
to Cappadocia, which is known to have had political relations
both with Syria and Israel in the ninth century B.C. (a king of
this northern Muṣri fought in alliance with Ahab and Ben-hadad
at the battle of Ḳarḳar in 854 B.C.). A combination of these
two northern powers for the relief of Samaria is conceivable at
this time, and the possibility of such might well give rise to the
events described in our text.

9. punishment will overtake us : lit. 'guilt will find us,'
i.e. we shall incur blame.

10. the porter : read 'porters' (so margin), i.e. the warders
of the gate (cf. *v.* 11).

told them, saying, We came to the camp of the Syrians,
and, behold, there was no man there, neither voice of
man, but the horses tied, and the asses tied, and the tents
as they were. And he called the porters; and they told 11
it to the king's household within. And the king arose in 12
the night, and said unto his servants, I will now shew you
what the Syrians have done to us. They know that we
be hungry; therefore are they gone out of the camp to
hide themselves in the field, saying, When they come out
of the city, we shall take them alive, and get into the city.
And one of his servants answered and said, Let some 13
take, I pray thee, five of the horses that remain, which
are left in the city, (behold, they are as all the multitude
of Israel that are left in it; behold, they are as all the
multitude of Israel that are consumed :) and let us send
and see. They took therefore two chariots with horses; 14
and the king sent after the host of the Syrians, saying, Go
and see. And they went after them unto Jordan: and, lo, 15
all the way was full of garments and vessels, which the
Syrians had cast away in their haste. And the messengers
returned, and told the king. And the people went out, 16
and spoiled the camp of the Syrians. So a measure of
fine flour was *sold* for a shekel, and two measures of
barley for a shekel, according to the word of the LORD.

---

11. And he called the porters: read, with LXX (Luc.) and
Targum, 'and the porters called.'

12. take them alive: cf. 1 Kings xx. 18.

13. five: a round number denoting a few, as in 1 Sam. xxi.
3 ('five loaves of bread'); Is. xix. 18, xxx. 17.

which are left in the city: the text has suffered from scribal
errors and repetitions (cf. LXX). This clause should be
omitted, and the parenthetic sentence that follows, in its
original form, probably read: ('behold they are as all the
multitude that are consumed'), i.e. the few surviving horses will
soon perish, under existing circumstances, like all the rest; they
may, therefore, well be risked in the present enterprise.

15. vessels: or 'weapons.'

and told the king: what the messengers reported showed
decisively that the retreat of the Syrians was not feigned.

17 And the king appointed the captain on whose hand he
leaned to have the charge of the gate: and the people
trode upon him in the gate, and he died as the man of
God had said, who spake when the king came down to
18 him. And it came to pass, as the man of God had spoken
to the king, saying, Two measures of barley for a shekel,
and a measure of fine flour for a shekel, shall be to-
19 morrow about this time in the gate of Samaria ; and that
captain answered the man of God, and said, Now, behold,
if the LORD should make windows in heaven, might such
a thing be? and he said, Behold, thou shalt see it with
20 thine eyes, but shalt not eat thereof: it came to pass
even so unto him ; for the people trode upon him in the
gate, and he died.

VIII. 1–15. THE ELISHA-NARRATIVES CONTINUED.

viii. 1–6. *Further help given to the Shunammite.*

8   Now Elisha had spoken unto the woman, whose son he
had restored to life, saying, Arise, and go thou and thine
household, and sojourn wheresoever thou canst sojourn:
for the LORD hath called for a famine ; and it shall also
2 come upon the land seven years. And the woman arose,

---

17. to have the charge of the gate : in order to maintain order
as the crowd surged out of the city, or possibly as they returned,
after having satisfied themselves with the spoils, from the Syrian
camp.   Not improbably, however, ' gate ' may here = market-
place, and the crush may have been that of eager buyers, from
the city, of corn and barley.
    as the man of God...spake : read 'according to the word of
the man of God which he spake ' etc.
    18–20.   These verses are probably a later addition. They
simply repeat and expand what has already been said.
    viii. 1–6.   Certain linguistic peculiarities show that this
section is connected with the narrative in ch. iv. It not improbably followed ch. iv. originally, and belongs to the same
source.
    1. sojourn...sojourn : i.e. sojourn wherever you can (no
particular place being specified)—a common idiom in the Semitic
languages.

and did according to the word of the man of God : and she went with her household, and sojourned in the land of the Philistines seven years. And it came to pass at **3** the seven years' end, that the woman returned out of the land of the Philistines : and she went forth to cry unto the king for her house and for her land. Now the king **4** was talking with Gehazi the servant of the man of God, saying, Tell me, I pray thee, all the great things that Elisha hath done. And it came to pass, as he was telling **5** the king how he had restored to life him that was dead, that, behold, the woman, whose son he had restored to life, cried to the king for her house and for her land. And Gehazi said, My lord, O king, this is the woman, and this is her son, whom Elisha restored to life. And **6** when the king asked the woman, she told him. So the king appointed unto her a certain officer, saying, Restore all that was hers, and all the fruits of the field since the day that she left the land, even until now.

---

2. in the land of the Philistines : cf. Gen. xxvi. 1. The Philistine lowlands were less subject to drought than the central highlands.

seven years : here again the number may be a round one. The 'seven years' famine' may be a popular way of describing one that lasted an unusually long time.

3. for her house and for her land : which had been taken possession of unlawfully by others. By the irony of circumstance she was now compelled to appeal to the king for help ; contrast iv. 13.

4. Gehazi could not have been a leper at this time—a leper would hardly have gained access to the Israelite king (though Naaman was apparently admitted to the royal palace, v. 6). Chapter v. narrates events subsequent to what is here told.

Tell me etc.: the stories of Elijah and Elisha had often, doubtless, been told in popular form before they were written down.

5. him that was dead : LXX 'a child that had died.'

6. all the fruits : or rather ' produce.' Possibly the estate had reverted to the royal domains during the interval. It is now restored, together with compensation equivalent to its annual revenue during the period of alienation.

viii. 7-15.   *Elisha and Hazael.*

7   And Elisha came to Damascus; and Ben-hadad the
king of Syria was sick; and it was told him, saying, The
8 man of God is come hither.   And the king said unto
Hazael, Take a present in thine hand, and go meet the
man of God, and inquire of the LORD by him, saying,
9 Shall I recover of this sickness?   So Hazael went to
meet him, and took a present with him, even of every
good thing of Damascus, forty camels' burden, and came

7-15.   The following section is fragmentary.   In the source
from which it was taken there probably existed some further
account of Hazael, and, perhaps, of a divine command to Elisha
to anoint Hazael king of Damascus.   According to 1 Kings xix.
15 Elijah had been commissioned to go to Damascus and anoint
Hazael king over Syria—a commission which he, apparently,
failed to execute.   Though Elisha predicts his accession to the
throne, no actual anointing of Hazael by the prophet is recorded.
Hazael himself is mentioned twice as king of Damascus in the
inscription of Shalmaneser II preserved on the Black Obelisk,
which is now in the British Museum.   The years indicated are
842 and 839 B.C.   It is clear from the present passage (and from
1 Kings xix. 15 f.) that he was not the legitimate heir to the
throne, but a usurper, probably as the result of a military conspiracy.

7.   came to Damascus: for what purpose the narrative, in
its present form, fails to state.   Doubtless he went in obedience
to a divine command.

Ben-hadad: i.e. the Ben-hadad who attacked Ahab without
success (1 Kings xx. 1).   As Hazael and Jehu were contemporary
kings, the incident here recorded must have taken place in the
reign of Jehoram.

The man of God is come etc.: Elisha is now, it would seem,
well known in Damascus as a man of God; contrast ch. v.
The healing of Naaman probably made his fame known in
Syria.

8.   inquire of the Lord: the sick king desired to have an
oracle from Jehovah by Jehovah's prophet.

Shall I recover etc.: cf. i. 2.

9.   a present...forty camels' burden: Damascus was a rich
emporium of commerce, being the centre of traffic between
Arabia and Eastern and Western Asia.   The costliness and
magnificence of the gift match the city's wealth.   At the same
time it must be remembered that Orientals love to make an
imposing but unnecessary display in bestowing presents.

and stood before him, and said, Thy son Ben-hadad king
of Syria hath sent me to thee, saying, Shall I recover of
this sickness? And Elisha said unto him, Go, say unto 10
him, Thou shalt surely recover; howbeit the LORD hath
shewed me that he shall surely die. And he settled his 11
countenance stedfastly *upon him*, until he was ashamed:
and the man of God wept. And Hazael said, Why 12
weepeth my lord? And he answered, Because I know
the evil that thou wilt do unto the children of Israel:
their strong holds wilt thou set on fire, and their young
men wilt thou slay with the sword, and wilt dash in pieces
their little ones, and rip up their women with child. And 13
Hazael said, But what is thy servant, which is but a dog,
that he should do this great thing? And Elisha answered,

---

10. Thou shalt surely recover; howbeit etc.: Elisha's
answer seems to be intended for Hazael rather than his master.
There is an ironical ring in his words. The prophet pierces
Hazael's treacherous design, and ironically bids him tell his
master he will recover, but adds that he (the prophet) knows
well that the issue will be otherwise—Ben-hadad will die (? by
Hazael's own hand). This interpretation is confirmed by what
follows in *vv.* 11 f.; notice especially Hazael's deprecating tone
in *v.* 13.

11. And he settled his countenance etc.: i.e. he stared
Hazael out of countenance. 'Hazael, conscious that Elisha had
read his thoughts aright, shrank from that piercing gaze ' (Ball).
But the correctness of this interpretation is uncertain. With a
slight change of pointing (partly supported by the LXX) the
Hebrew may be rendered: 'And his face became fixed and
unutterably amazed,' i.e. took on a set look of extreme amaze-
ment and horror. In this case the sentence describes Elisha's
appearance in the prophetic ecstasy, when the future havoc, to
be wrought by Hazael on Israel, is revealed to him.

12. their strong holds etc.: the sentence gives a vivid
description of the horrors of warfare as practised at the time;
cf. iii. 25, xv. 16, and esp. Amos i. 3, 13.

13. But what is thy servant etc.: lit. 'thy servant the dog';
Hazael answers in a tone of exaggerated humility. He is all too
poor a creature to be able to accomplish such great things. It
must be remembered he was not the legitimate heir of the
throne.

The LORD hath shewed me that thou shalt be king over
14 Syria.   Then he departed from Elisha, and came to his
master; who said to him, What said Elisha to thee?   And
he answered, He told me that thou shouldest surely re-
15 cover.   And it came to pass on the morrow, that he took
the coverlet, and dipped it in water, and spread it on his
face, so that he died: and Hazael reigned in his stead.

VIII. 16–24. JEHORAM OF JUDAH (cf. 2 Chron. xxi.).

viii. 16–19. *Introduction.*

16   And in the fifth year of Joram the son of Ahab king of
Israel, Jehoshaphat being then king of Judah, Jehoram
the son of Jehoshaphat king of Judah began to reign.
17 Thirty and two years old was he when he began to reign;
18 and he reigned eight years in Jerusalem.   And he walked
in the way of the kings of Israel, as did the house of
Ahab: for he had the daughter of Ahab to wife: and he

The Lord hath shewed me etc.: lit. 'hath caused me to see
thee (? in the prophetic trance) as king over Syria.'
  15. the coverlet: the meaning of the Hebrew word so
translated is uncertain.   It is evident, from the fact that it was
dipped in water and then laid on the face of the king, that it
denotes some kind of cloth with which the king was suffocated.
  16–24. The introduction (*vv.* 16–19) and also *vv.* 23, 24 are
the work of the compiler; the middle section (*vv.* 20–22) is an
extract from the chronicles of Judah.   The usual arrangement of
the material, however, is not adhered to in this case.   We should
expect the account of the reign of Jehoram of Israel to be con-
cluded before the introduction of the contemporary kings of
Judah.   These (Jehoram and Ahaziah of Judah) are dealt with
first in order to lead up to the account of Jehu's revolution,
which was inaugurated by the death, on the same day, of a king
of Israel and a king of Judah.
  16.   Joram is the shorter form of **Jehoram**; both forms appear
to be used indiscriminately.
  Jehoshaphat being then king of Judah: omit with LXX.
The words are obviously a scribal error.
  18.   the daughter of Ahab: Athaliah (cf. *v.* 26, xi. 1).   The
fact that he was son-in-law of Ahab and Jezebel will explain

did that which was evil in the sight of the LORD. How- 19
beit the LORD would not destroy Judah, for David his
servant's sake, as he promised him to give unto him a
lamp for his children alway.

viii. 20–22. *Revolt of Edom and Libnah.*

In his days Edom revolted from under the hand of 20
Judah, and made a king over themselves. Then Joram 21
passed over to Zair, and all his chariots with him: and
he rose up by night, and smote the Edomites which
compassed him about, and the captains of the chariots:
and the people fled to their tents. So Edom revolted 22

why ' he walked in the way of the kings of Israel, as did the
house of Ahab,' i.e. countenanced the worship of the Tyrian
Baal, which was so offensive to the prophetic party. Note that
the hated name of the queen-mother is omitted.

19. for David his servant's sake: cf. 2 Sam. vii. 12–16.

a lamp for his children: read 'a lamp before him' (cf.
1 Kings xi. 36); the children are themselves the lamp. The
'lamp' is a figure for continued life (cf. Job xviii. 5, 6, 'his
lamp...shall be put out'; Prov. xiii. 9, xx. 20; 2 Chron. xxi. 7).
It is an Eastern custom to keep a lamp constantly burning in the
home, and its extinction signifies that the home has ceased to
be. According to ancient ideas a man lived on in his posterity.

20. and made a king: cf. iii. 9, where Edom's vassal
position is implied. See also 1 Kings xxii. 47. Edom seems to
have been a vassal-state of Judah since the time of Rehoboam.

21. Zair: not otherwise known. Conder has suggested its
identification with *es-Zuwēra*, at the south-west end of the Dead
Sea. The Vulg. has 'Seir.'

all his chariots with him : and he rose up: the text is in
disorder; between 'with him' and 'and he rose up' some
words describing how he fell into an ambush have probably
fallen out. 'And he rose up by night' etc. will then describe
how he cut his way through the surrounding force and saved
part of his army by flight.

and the captains of the chariots: as 'the captains of the
chariots' are evidently Joram's own, he can hardly have smitten
them; read (with a very slight change) 'and with him were the
captains of the chariots.'

from under the hand of Judah, unto this day.   Then did
Libnah revolt at the same time.

viii. 23-24.   *Concluding notice of the reign of Jehoram*
(Joram) of Judah.

23 And the rest of the acts of Joram, and all that he did,
are they not written in the book of the chronicles of the
24 kings of Judah?   And Joram slept with his fathers, and
was buried with his fathers in the city of David: and
Ahaziah his son reigned in his stead.

VIII. 25-29.   AHAZIAH OF JUDAH.

viii. 25-27.   *Introduction.*

25   In the twelfth year of Joram the son of Ahab king of
Israel did Ahaziah the son of Jehoram king of Judah

---

22.   unto this day: this phrase was probably added by the
Deuteronomic compiler.

Libnah: Libnah occupied a position of strategical importance on the lowland plain, probably south-west of Judah.
According to Eusebius it lay in the district of Eleutheropolis (the
present *Beit Jibrin*); in 2 Kings xix. 8 Libnah and Lachish are
mentioned together.   Libnah apparently took advantage of
Edom's successful revolt to assert its own independence.   It
may have been involved in the Philistine and Arabian attack
on Judah recorded in 2 Chron. xxi. 16 f.; and, in any case, its
population was probably non-Israelitish.   In Hezekiah's reign
(cf. xix. 8, xxiii. 31, xxiv. 18) it was again a dependency of
Judah.

24.   with his fathers etc.: but according to 2 Chron xxi. 20
he was not buried in the royal tombs.

25-29.   This section is wholly the work of the Deuteronomic
compiler.   The notice of the king's death is postponed in order
that it may be described in connexion with the revolution of
Jehu.

25.   twelfth: the LXX (Luc.) has 'eleventh,' which agrees
with ix. 29.   In the usual chronological scheme part of a year is
reckoned as one year; hence, because Ahaziah reigned but one
year (cf. *v.* 26), to have said that he began to reign in the
eleventh year of Joram—who reigned altogether twelve years—
would have made it necessary to extend his reign to two years.
Consequently 'eleventh' has been altered in the present notice
to 'twelfth.'

begin to reign.   Two and twenty years old was Ahaziah 26
when he began to reign ; and he reigned one year in
Jerusalem.   And his mother's name was Athaliah the
daughter of Omri king of Israel.   And he walked in the 27
way of the house of Ahab, and did that which was evil in
the sight of the LORD, as did the house of Ahab : for he
was the son in law of the house of Ahab.

viii. 28–29.   *The war with Hazael* (cf. ix. 14, 15).

And he went with Joram the son of Ahab to war against 28
Hazael king of Syria at Ramoth-gilead : and the Syrians
wounded Joram.   And king Joram returned to be healed 29
in Jezreel of the wounds which the Syrians had given him
at Ramah, when he fought against Hazael king of Syria.
And Ahaziah the son of Jehoram king of Judah went
down to see Joram the son of Ahab in Jezreel, because he
was sick.

IX., X. 1–27.   THE REVOLUTION OF JEHU.

ix. 1–13.   *Jehu anointed king.*

And Elisha the prophet called one of the sons of the 9
prophets, and said unto him, Gird up thy loins, and take

---

26.   daughter : here = ' granddaughter ' (R.V. margin) ; cf.
v. 18 ; possibly it has the general sense of 'descendant.'   Omri
is mentioned as the famous founder of the dynasty.

27.   for he was the son in law...Ahab : LXX omits.   Strictly
he was Ahab's grandson.   The parallel in 2 Chron. substitutes
for this clause, 'for his mother was his counsellor to do
wickedly.'

28.   Ramoth-gilead : cf. note on ix. 1.

29.   Jezreel was the seat of the court at this time ; cf. x. 11
and 13 (and notes).

Ahaziah...went down : i.e. (probably) from Jerusalem.   This
implies that the Judaean king was not at the seat of war ; cf.
ix. 15.

ix., x.   The long and powerful narrative contained in
chs. ix. and x. has been extracted almost wholly from an old
source, the hand of the compiler only becoming occasionally
visible (cf. ix. 7–10, 14–15, x. 28–36).   It may be compared, in
its wealth of detail and vivid delineation, with 1 Kings xx. and

this vial of oil in thine hand, and go to Ramoth-gilead.
2 And when thou comest thither, look out there Jehu the
son of Jehoshaphat the son of Nimshi, and go in, and
make him arise up from among his brethren, and carry
3 him to an inner chamber.   Then take the vial of oil, and

---

xxii., and may, indeed, have been derived from the same popular
history, though some scholars doubt this.

The tragic events described mark the climax of a long period
of opposition, on the part of the prophetic party (an opposition
begun by Elijah) to the religious policy of the house of Omri.
The overthrow of the reigning house, and the extirpation of the
Baal-worship are ruthlessly effected by Jehu, a military officer
of extraordinary energy in the Israelitish army.   Though the
military revolution was directly promoted by Elisha, the wholesale massacres which accompanied it seem to have excited a
widespread feeling of horror that made itself felt in prophetic
circles also (cf. Hosea i. 4).   It is possible that some sections in
the narrative are not in their original order, and there appear to
be occasional traces of omission.

ix. 1.   to Ramoth-gilead : the possession of this stronghold
was disputed between Israel and Syria, and Ahab lost his life in
a vain attempt to recover it (cf. 1 Kings xxii.).   At the time
referred to in this chapter it was being held by the Israelite army
against the Syrians.   The king (Jehoram) had, however, retired
to Jezreel wounded.   The site of the city has not been fixed.
It must have been considerably further north than *es-Salt*—a
town about eighteen miles north of the Dead Sea—with which it
is commonly identified.

2.   Jehu : in *v.* 20 and also 1 Kings xix. 16 Jehu is called
'son of Nimshi,' who, according to the present verse, was his
grandfather.   The latter may have been a more important
personage than his father Jehoshaphat.   Nothing further is
known of his origin.   Jehu is twice mentioned by Shalmaneser II
as one of his tributaries.   In one of these inscriptions (that on
the Black Obelisk) there is a representation of an embassy of
tribute-bearers kneeling before the Assyrian king, with the super-
scription, ' Tribute of Ya'ua (Jehu) son of Omri.'   That Jehu,
the exterminator of Omri's dynasty, should be called 'son of
Omri ' in the Assyrian inscriptions is remarkable.   It may be
explained by the fact that Omri, as the founder of a powerful
dynasty, enjoyed a high reputation in Assyria.   It was a
favourite Assyrian mode of speech to designate the successor of
a celebrated ruler as the 'son' of the latter.   Similarly Israel is
referred to as 'the land of the house of Omri.'

to an inner chamber : cf. 1 Kings xix. 30, xxii. 25.

pour it on his head, and say, Thus saith the LORD, I have anointed thee king over Israel. Then open the door, and flee, and tarry not. So the young man, even the young 4 man the prophet, went to Ramoth-gilead. And when he 5 came, behold, the captains of the host were sitting ; and he said, I have an errand to thee, O captain. And Jehu said, Unto which of all us ? And he said, To thee, O captain. And he arose, and went into the house ; and 6 he poured the oil on his head, and said unto him, Thus saith the LORD, the God of Israel, I have anointed thee king over the people of the LORD, even over Israel. And 7 thou shalt smite the house of Ahab thy master, that I may avenge the blood of my servants the prophets, and the blood of all the servants of the LORD, at the hand of Jezebel. For the whole house of Ahab shall perish : and 8 I will cut off from Ahab every man child, and him that is shut up and him that is left at large in Israel. And 9 I will make the house of Ahab like the house of Jeroboam the son of Nebat, and like the house of Baasha the son

---

3. I have anointed thee etc. : cf. 1 Kings i. 39 (the anointing of Solomon). The anointing was a solemn act of consecration ; a king thus became ' the anointed of the Lord,' and a sacred person.

5. were sitting : perhaps in council.

Unto which etc. : Jehu apparently is not in chief command. *vv.* 7–10*a* are an addition from the hand of the Deuteronomic compiler ; *v.* 10*b* ('and he opened the door and fled ') is the original sequel of *v.* 6.

7. the blood of my servants etc. : Jezebel's persecution of the prophets is alluded to in 1 Kings xviii. 4, 13 (' when Jezebel slew the prophets of the Lord') ; but no details have been preserved.

8. I will cut off from Ahab etc.: this clause is a repetition of 1 Kings xxi. 21 *b*. The expression ' him that is shut up and him that is left at large ' is a proverbial one = ' all,' everyone being regarded as included under one or other of the two categories.

9. like the house of Jeroboam etc. : for the extinction of Jeroboam's dynasty by Baasha cf. 1 Kings xv. 27 f. ; and for the downfall of Baasha cf. 1 Kings xvi. 3, 9 f.

10 of Ahijah. And the dogs shall eat Jezebel in the portion
of Jezreel, and there shall be none to bury her. And he
11 opened the door, and fled. Then Jehu came forth to the
servants of his lord: and one said unto him, Is all well?
wherefore came this mad fellow to thee? And he said
unto them, Ye know the man and what his talk was.
12 And they said, It is false; tell us now. And he said,
Thus and thus spake he to me, saying, Thus saith the
13 LORD, I have anointed thee king over Israel. Then they
hasted, and took every man his garment, and put it under
him on the top of the stairs, and blew the trumpet, saying,
Jehu is king.

---

10. the dogs shall eat Jezebel etc.: cf. Elijah's threat
1 Kings xxi. 23.

11. and one said: read, with LXX and the other Versions,
'and they said.'

this mad fellow: a prophet was still essentially an ecstatic,
and his actions in the ecstatic condition suggested those of a
madman. It must be remembered that madness, by the ancient
world, was attributed to supernatural influence. While there is
a shade of contempt in the use of 'madman' here, it must not
be exaggerated. Even a madman is regarded in the East with
a certain amount of superstitious reverence. Cf. Hos. ix. 7
('The prophet is a fool, the man that hath the spirit is mad ').

Ye know the man etc.: Jehu dismisses the matter with an
appearance of contempt—his fellow-officers know the sort of
talk indulged in by such fanatics. He pretends to evade the
question.

12. It is false: perhaps 'trickery' would be a better
rendering. A slight change in the Hebrew word would yield
the sense 'treason' ('conspiracy'); cf. xi. 14.

13. took...his garment etc.: they symbolize their homage
to the new king by placing their cloaks under Jehu's feet; cf.
Matt. xxi. 8. The words rendered 'on the top of the steps' are
difficult, and there may be some corruption in the text. A
slight change would yield the sense 'upon the elevation of the
steps'; or the words may be rendered 'on to the body of the
steps.' 'The stairway on the outside of the steps, leading to
the roof, served as an extemporised throne, or rather platform
for the king (cf. xi. 14) ' (Ball).

ix. 14-29. *The murder of Jehoram and Ahaziah.*

So Jehu the son of Jehoshaphat the son of Nimshi 14
conspired against Joram. (Now Joram kept Ramoth-
gilead, he and all Israel, because of Hazael king of Syria:
but king Joram was returned to be healed in Jezreel of 15
the wounds which the Syrians had given him, when he
fought with Hazael king of Syria.) And Jehu said, If
this be your mind, then let none escape and go forth out
of the city, to go to tell it in Jezreel. So Jehu rode in 16
a chariot, and went to Jezreel; for Joram lay there. And
Ahaziah king of Judah was come down to see Joram.
Now the watchman stood on the tower in Jezreel, and he 17
spied the company of Jehu as he came, and said, I see
a company. And Joram said, Take an horseman, and
send to meet them, and let him say, Is it peace? So there 18
went one on horseback to meet him, and said, Thus
saith the king, Is it peace? And Jehu said, What hast

---

14 b, 15. These verses form a parenthesis which is intended
to explain what follows: Jehu was at Ramoth-gilead, while
Joram had retired wounded to Jezreel (cf. viii. 28, 29). Possibly
the verses are an abridgement of a longer section in the original
document.

14. now Joram kept etc.: possibly 'Jehu' should be read
instead of 'Joram'; then render 'Now Jehu was on guard in
Ramoth-gilead ' etc.

15. let none escape etc.: rather 'let not a fugitive go forth,'
viz. out of the city. This shows that the Israelites were in
possession of Ramoth-gilead, and not besieging it. Jehu took
precautions that no swift messenger should get ahead of him
with news of his conspiracy.

16. And Ahaziah etc.: or rather 'now Ahaziah had come
down': again recapitulating; cp. viii. 29 *b*.

17. the watchman: the scene now shifts to Jezreel; 'the
tower' is one of the towers of the palace.

the company: the Hebrew word means 'abundance,' 'over-
flow' and so 'multitude': cf. Is. lx. 6; Ezek. xxvi. 10.

a company: probably a word has fallen out: read 'a company (multitude) of men.'

18. Is it peace? Or better, with the margin, 'Is all well?'
the customary salutation (cf. v. 21). The king did not till the

thou to do with peace? turn thee behind me. And the
watchman told, saying, The messenger came to them,
19 but he cometh not again. Then he sent out a second on
horseback, which came to them, and said, Thus saith the
king, Is it peace? And Jehu answered, What hast thou
20 to do with peace? turn thee behind me. And the watchman told, saying, He came even unto them, and cometh
not again: and the driving is like the driving of Jehu the
21 son of Nimshi; for he driveth furiously. And Joram
said, Make ready. And they made ready his chariot.
And Joram king of Israel and Ahaziah king of Judah
went out, each in his chariot, and they went out to meet
Jehu, and found him in the portion of Naboth the
22 Jezreelite. And it came to pass, when Joram saw Jehu,
that he said, Is it peace, Jehu? And he answered, What
peace, so long as the whoredoms of thy mother Jezebel

---

last (cf. *v.* 23) suspect treachery; the unexpected and sudden
arrival of Jehu rather suggested bad news from the front.

What hast thou to do with peace? Perhaps the meaning
may be paraphrased: 'What business have you to offer salutations and ask questions?' Burney, however, explains the
meaning thus: 'What hast thou (as an emissary of Ahab's son)
to do with peace?' i.e. there can be no question of peace so
long as the house of Ahab exists.

20. furiously, or 'madly': the Hebrew word is cognate to
that rendered 'mad fellow' in *v.* 11.

21. And Joram etc.: the kings would hardly have left the
protection of the palace walls, and have driven out without an
escort if they had suspected treachery.

in the portion of Naboth etc.: Naboth's vineyard now formed
part of the grounds of the palace; cf. 1 Kings xxi. 16.

22. Is it peace? or, rather, 'Is all well' (at the seat of
war)?

What peace etc.: or, perhaps (with a different vocalization),
'How (can it be) "Is all well" so long as' etc. 'Between us
there can be no greetings so long as the idolatry of Jezebel continues': so the Targum. Jehu proclaims himself the champion
of the legitimate religion of Jehovah against Jezebel and her
foreign Baal-worship.

whoredoms...witchcrafts: i.e. idolatry; apostasy from the
religion of Jehovah is 'whoredom' in the language of the

and her witchcrafts are so many? And Joram turned 23
his hands, and fled, and said to Ahaziah, There is
treachery, O Ahaziah. And Jehu drew his bow with his 24
full strength, and smote Joram between his arms, and
the arrow went out at his heart, and he sunk down in his
chariot. Then said *Jehu* to Bidkar his captain, Take up, 25
and cast him in the portion of the field of Naboth the
Jezreelite: for remember how that, when I and thou rode
together after Ahab his father, the LORD laid this burden
upon him; Surely I have seen yesterday the blood of 26
Naboth, and the blood of his sons, saith the LORD; and
I will requite thee in this plat, saith the LORD. Now
therefore take and cast him into the plat *of ground*, according to the word of the LORD. But when Ahaziah the 27
king of Judah saw this, he fled by the way of the garden
house. And Jehu followed after him, and said, Smite

---

prophets (cf. Hosea i. and ii.); 'witchcrafts' in the form of
sorcery (spells, enchantments) was a common feature in Semitic
heathen religions.

23. turned his hands: i.e. turned his horses round; cf. 1 Kings
xxii. 34 ('said to the driver, Turn thine hand').

24. drew his bow etc.: or, rather (cf. margin), 'had filled his
hand with the bow,' i.e. had prepared to shoot, holding the bow
ready in his hand.

25. his captain: or, rather, 'adjutant'; cf. vii. 2.

for remember etc.: read, with LXX (Luc.), Vulg. and Syriac,
'for I remember how I and thou' etc.

laid this burden: or, rather, 'uttered this (prophetic) oracle.'
The word rendered 'burden' is often used to describe the oracles
of the prophets; cf. Is. xiii. 1; Mal. i. 1 etc.

26. Surely etc.: the oracle, uttered by Elijah, is given in
a different form in 1 Kings xxi. 19; the form given here is
probably more original. The two narratives are probably independent and embody independent traditions. In 1 Kings xxi.
Naboth's sons are not said to have been put to death.

plat: or 'portion' (the same word as in *v.* 25 etc.).

27. the garden house: this should probably be read as a
place-name, *Beth ha-gan* (the *En-gannim* of Josh. xix. 21); it
is plausibly identified with the modern *Jenin*, lying on the south
side of the plain of Jezreel, on the high road to Jerusalem
(Benzinger).

him also in the chariot: *and they smote him* at the ascent
of Gur, which is by Ibleam. And he fled to Megiddo, and
28 died there. And his servants carried him in a chariot to
Jerusalem, and buried him in his sepulchre with his fathers
in the city of David.

29   And in the eleventh year of Joram the son of Ahab
began Ahaziah to reign over Judah.

ix. 30–37. *The death of Jezebel.*

30   And when Jehu was come to Jezreel, Jezebel heard of
it; and she painted her eyes, and tired her head, and
31 looked out at the window. And as Jehu entered in at the
gate, she said, Is it peace, thou Zimri, thy master's
32 murderer? And he lifted up his face to the window, and

Ibleam (in 1 Chron. vi. 70 'Bileam'), the modern *Bel‘anne*,
lay between Jezreel and Megiddo (a short distance south of
Jenin). The 'ascent of Gur,' which lay in the immediate neighbourhood, is not mentioned elsewhere.

Megiddo, the modern *Lejjun* (probably), occupied a position
of considerable strategical importance in the south of the plain
of Jezreel. It was a strong fortress, and lay about eleven miles
north-west of *Jenin*. In 2 Chron. xxii. 9 a different tradition
as to Ahaziah's death is given.

29. This *v.*, which is obviously redactional in character,
breaks the connexion in its present context. For **the eleventh
year** cf. viii. 25 and note (it agrees with the chronology of the
Lucianic recension of the LXX). The *v.* is the introduction to
a summary notice of Ahaziah's reign, which may originally have
stood here (in its full form) in some MSS.

30. And when Jehu was come: or, rather, 'And Jehu came'
(i.e. after the wounding of Ahaziah).

painted her eyes: lit. 'set her eyes in *stibium* (or antimony)';
the *kohl* of the Arabs, a black powder which is mixed with oil
and used by Eastern women to paint the eye-lashes and brows,
the effect being to give brilliancy to and enhance the apparent
size of the eyes.

tired: i.e. adorned with a tire or head-dress.

31. Is it peace etc.: an ironical greeting: 'is all well?'
note the sarcasm in calling Jehu a second Zimri, destined to
enjoy as brief a tenure of power as that regicide (cf. 1 Kings
xvi. 15–18).

said, Who is on my side? who? And there looked out
to him two or three eunuchs. And he said, Throw her 33
down. So they threw her down: and some of her blood
was sprinkled on the wall, and on the horses: and he
trode her under foot. And when he was come in, he did 34
eat and drink; and he said, See now to this cursed
woman, and bury her: for she is a king's daughter. And 35
they went to bury her: but they found no more of her
than the skull, and the feet, and the palms of her hands.
Wherefore they came again, and told him. And he said, 36
This is the word of the LORD, which he spake by his
servant Elijah the Tishbite, saying, In the portion
of Jezreel shall the dogs eat the flesh of Jezebel: and the 37
carcase of Jezebel shall be as dung upon the face of the
field in the portion of Jezreel; so that they shall not say,
This is Jezebel.

x. 1–14. *Murder of the princes of the royal houses of Israel
and Judah.*

Now Ahab had seventy sons in Samaria. And Jehu **10**
wrote letters, and sent to Samaria, unto the rulers of
Jezreel, even the elders, and unto them that brought up

---

32. **Who is on my side? who?** The LXX has a different
reading, on the basis of which Klostermann deduces the text:
'who art thou [murderess as thou art] that thou wouldest con-
tend with me?' This yields an excellent sense.

33. **and he trode**: read, with the Versions, 'and they (i.e.
the horses) trode' etc.

34. **cursed**: i.e. cursed by Elijah; see next verse.

a king's daughter: cf. 1 Kings xvi. 31.

36. **This is the word** etc.: cf. 1 Kings xxi. 23.

x. 1. **seventy sons**: 'sons' here may = descendants (of the
house of Ahab). Some scholars think that 'seventy' in this
connexion is a round number: cf. Judges viii. 30 f.

unto the rulers...elders: read, with LXX (Luc.), 'to the
rulers of the city and to the elders'; the 'rulers' are the officials
of the city, and the 'elders' the representatives of the people.

them that brought up: 'guardians' would be a better rendering (the Hebrew word is translated 'foster-father' in Numb.
xi. 12; Is. xlix. 23). The descendants of the house of Ahab

2 *the sons of* Ahab, saying, And now as soon as this letter
cometh to you, seeing your master's sons are with you,
and there are with you chariots and horses, a fenced city
3 also, and armour; look ye out the best and meetest of
your master's sons, and set him on his father's throne,
4 and fight for your master's house. But they were exceedingly afraid, and said, Behold, the two kings stood
5 not before him : how then shall we stand ? And he that
was over the household, and he that was over the city,
the elders also, and they that brought up *the children*,
sent to Jehu, saying, We are thy servants, and will do all
that thou shalt bid us ; we will not make any man king :
6 do thou that which is good in thine eyes. Then he wrote
a letter the second time to them, saying, If ye be on my
side, and if ye will hearken unto my voice, take ye the
heads of the men your master's sons, and come to me to
Jezreel by to-morrow this time. Now the king's sons,
being seventy persons, were with the great men of the
7 city, which brought them up. And it came to pass, when
the letter came to them, that they took the king's sons,
and slew them, even seventy persons, and put their heads
8 in baskets, and sent them unto him to Jezreel. And there

(including Jehoram's sons) had been placed, apparently, under
the supervision of certain nobles in Samaria, who were responsible for their good behaviour.

2. And now etc.: the last and principal part of the letter
only is cited, as in v. 6. Jehu ironically challenges a fight for
the dynasty.

a fenced city: the Versions have 'fenced cities.'

5. he that was over the household: i.e. the prefect of the
palace.

he...city: i.e. the governor of the city; cf. 1 Kings xxii. 26.
These two were the highest officials in the city.

6. and come to me: read, with LXX, 'and bring them to
me.'

7. and slew: 'butchered' would correctly represent the
Hebrew word used. The writer evidently did not sympathize
with Jehu's methods of wholesale slaughter.

came a messenger, and told him, saying, They have
brought the heads of the king's sons. And he said, Lay
ye them in two heaps at the entering in of the gate until
the morning. And it came to pass in the morning, that 9
he went out, and stood, and said to all the people, Ye be
righteous: behold, I conspired against my master, and
slew him: but who smote all these? Know now that 10
there shall fall unto the earth nothing of the word of the
LORD, which the LORD spake concerning the house of
Ahab: for the LORD hath done that which he spake by
his servant Elijah. So Jehu smote all that remained of 11
the house of Ahab in Jezreel, and all his great men, and
his familiar friends, and his priests, until he left him none
remaining. And he arose and departed, and went to 12
Samaria. And as he was at the shearing house of the

---

9. Ye be righteous etc.: 'righteous,' as often, has the
meaning 'guiltless' here, i.e. in respect of the massacre. Evidently the wholesale butchery had created a feeling of horror
and dismay among the people. Jehu now tries to reassure them
by telling them that both he and themselves are innocent of
any complicity in the massacre; for himself he accepts responsi-
bility for the murder of Jehoram alone. Jehu assumes that the
people know who have actually butchered the princes, but not
that he himself was the instigator.

10. Know now etc.: and, after all, what has happened is
but the fulfilment of the prophetic word spoken by Elijah; cf.
1 Kings xxi. 21. The circumstances have been overruled by
Providence.

11. So Jehu smote: rather 'And Jehu smote'; the verse
relates further massacres. Not only members of the royal house,
but all who were in any way prominently identified with it
(palace officials, priests etc.) suffered. For **all his great men**
read, with LXX (Luc.), 'all his kinsmen' (lit. 'redeemers,' i.e.
those to whom pertained the duties of kinsmen, especially that
of the blood-avenger): cf. 1 Kings xvi. 11.

12. And he arose...went: read 'And Jehu arose and went.'
the shearing house of the shepherds: margin, 'house of
gathering.' Both renderings are conjectural. Whether a place
or an isolated building 'which served as a *rendezvous* for the
shepherds of the neighbourhood' (Ball) be meant is uncertain.
The LXX treats it as a place-name 'Beth-Eked of the shepherds.'
In any case the locality intended is not known. It cannot be

13 shepherds in the way, Jehu met with the brethren of
Ahaziah king of Judah, and said, Who are ye? And they
answered, We are the brethren of Ahaziah : and we go
down to salute the children of the king and the children
14 of the queen.   And he said, Take them alive.   And they
took them alive, and slew them at the pit of the shearing
house, even two and forty men ; neither left he any of
them.

x. 15, 16.   Jehu and Jehonadab.

15   And when he was departed thence, he lighted on
Jehonadab the son of Rechab coming to meet him : and

---

identified with *Beth-Ḳad* (about six miles east of *Jenin*), which
is too far off the road from Jezreel to Samaria.   Possibly the
text is corrupt.   The context would seem to require a locality
south of Samaria.

13. the brethren of Ahaziah etc.: i.e. Ahaziah's kinsmen.
According to 2 Chron. xxii. 1 (cf. xxi. 17) Ahaziah's own
brothers had all perished in an Arab raid during the life-time
of his father Jehoram.

we go down: rather 'we have gone down.'   It has been
suggested that the incident here described really took place as
the kinsmen of Ahaziah were on their way home after a visit
to king Joram and the queen-mother, Jezebel, at Jezreel.   If
so, their ignorance of what had happened *after their visit*
would be explained.   The verses may not be in their original
position.

the king...the queen: i.e. Joram and Jezebel (the 'children'
of the latter would be Joram's brothers).

14. Take them alive: cf. 1 Kings xx. 18.

slew them: 'butchered them,' presumably as being connected with the doomed house of Ahab.

at the pit of the shearing house: or rather 'at the cistern
of Beth-Eḳed' (cf. *v.* 12 and note): 'pit' is omitted by LXX
(Luc.).

15. Jehonadab the son of Rechab: or rather 'Jehonadab
the Rechabite' ('son of Rechab' = Rechabite, just as 'son of a
prophet' = prophet).   This Jehonadab (or ?Rechab)[1] was the
reputed 'father'—i.e. the founder—of the Rechabite order,
which was still in existence in the later years of the Judaean

---

[1] The general editor suggests that the *founder* of an order like that of the
Rechabites, perhaps as primitive as the Nazirites, can hardly be looked for
so late as Jonadab.

he saluted him, and said to him, Is thine heart right, as my heart is with thy heart? And Jehonadab answered, It is. If it be, give me thine hand. And he gave him his hand; and he took him up to him into the chariot. And he said, Come with me, and see my zeal for the 16 Lord. So they made him ride in his chariot.

x. 17–27. *Extirpation of the Baal-worship.*

And when he came to Samaria, he smote all that re- 17 mained unto Ahab in Samaria, till he had destroyed him, according to the word of the Lord, which he spake to Elijah. And Jehu gathered all the people together, and 18 said unto them, Ahab served Baal a little; but Jehu shall serve him much. Now therefore call unto me all the 19 prophets of Baal, all his worshippers, and all his priests;

monarchy (cf. Jer. xxxv., especially *v.* 6). The movement was a protest against the corruption of the old simple ideals of Hebrew life which had come in with the growth of a more settled civilization. Its adherents bound themselves to abstain from wine, from dwelling in houses, and from the practice of agriculture; it aimed in fact at reviving the old simple nomadic life. With agriculture and city-life had come the corrupting influence of Baal-worship; the two seemed inseparable. Jehonadab would inevitably be in violent opposition to Jezebel and her foreign innovations, and his alliance with Jehu would there-fore be quite a natural proceeding. For the work of extirpating foreign idolatry he was willing, for the time being, to abandon his attitude of aloofness and take an active part in political affairs. 'Rechabite' may possibly have meant originally 'member of a band of riders' (? with reference to their nomadic way of life).

Is thine heart...thy heart? Read, with LXX (Luc.), 'Is thy heart right (i.e. rightly) with my heart, as my heart is with thy heart?' Jehonadab's answer consists of: **It is.**

If it be etc.: these words belong to Jehu's reply; this is made clear in the LXX which adds 'And Jehu said': Jeho-nadab is treated by Jehu as a person of far-reaching influence, whose co-operation it was important to secure.

16. they made him ride: read 'he made him ride with him.'

19. all the prophets...priests: probably the words 'all his worshippers' should be omitted. Jehu first summons the

let none be wanting: for I have a great sacrifice *to do* to
Baal; whosoever shall be wanting, he shall not live.
But Jehu did it in subtilty, to the intent that he might
20 destroy the worshippers of Baal. And Jehu said, Sanctify
a solemn assembly for Baal. And they proclaimed it.
21 And Jehu sent through all Israel: and all the worshippers
of Baal came, so that there was not a man left that came
not. And they came into the house of Baal; and the
22 house of Baal was filled from one end to another. And
he said unto him that was over the vestry, Bring forth
vestments for all the worshippers of Baal. And he
23 brought them forth vestments. And Jehu went, and
Jehonadab the son of Rechab, into the house of Baal;
and he said unto the worshippers of Baal, Search, and
look that there be here with you none of the servants of
24 the LORD, but the worshippers of Baal only. And they
went in to offer sacrifices and burnt offerings. Now Jehu
had appointed him fourscore men without, and said, If
any of the men whom I bring into your hands escape, *he*

---

priests and prophets of Baal, in order that through them the
people may be summoned to a festival in the temple of Baal.
It is difficult to imagine how so transparent a device could have
succeeded. Possibly the Baal-worshippers obeyed the summons
out of sheer terror, hoping for the best.

19. call...the prophets of Baal: cf. 1 Kings xviii. 19 f.

20. a solemn assembly: i.e. a solemn assembly in honour
of Baal (a gathering for religious purposes); the term is sometimes used in this general sense (cf. Is. i. 13; Amos v. 22),
but often in a special sense of the gathering of pilgrims for
certain feasts (cf. Deut. xvi. 8; Lev. xxv. 36 etc.).

22. the vestry or 'wardrobe': the word occurs here only.
The wardrobe of the Baal-temple is apparently meant. It was
customary to put on festal attire for sacred occasions. In those
cases where the people were too poor to have special garments
for this purpose, their ordinary clothes were washed (both before
and after the ceremony). Apparently a supply of festal garments
was kept in the Baal-temple.

24. And they went in: read with LXX 'and he went in':
Jehu alone offers his sacrifice, as *v.* 25 *a* shows.

If any...men etc.: render (with a difference of vocalization in

that letteth him go, his life shall be for the life of him. And 25
it came to pass, as soon as he had made an end of
offering the burnt offering, that Jehu said to the guard
and to the captains, Go in, and slay them; let none come
forth. And they smote them with the edge of the sword;
and the guard and the captains cast them out, and went
to the city of the house of Baal. And they brought forth 26
the pillars that were in the house of Baal, and burned
them. And they brake down the pillar of Baal, and 27
brake down the house of Baal, and made it a draught
house, unto this day.

---

one Hebrew word): 'the man who suffers any of those men to
escape whom I bring to you, his life' etc.

25. to the guard and to the captains: the royal body-guard
and its officers is probably meant.

and the guard...cast them out: i.e. cast out the corpses;
but no object is expressed in the original. The repetition of
'the guard' etc. is also strange. There is probably some corruption in the text.

to the city of the house of Baal: this rendering yields no
intelligible sense. The word translated 'city' must be corrupt:
read 'and went to (i.e. entered) the inner shrine of the house of
Baal.'

26. the pillars: LXX (Luc.) 'pillar' (sing.); but a pillar,
being of stone, could not be burnt; therefore the text should
probably be corrected to 'asherah'; then read: 'and they
brought forth the asherah of the house of Baal and burnt it':
cf. 1 Kings xvi. 32, 33 (where Ahab is said to have erected
an asherah in connexion with the Baal-worship), and 2 Kings
xxiii. 6.

27. the pillar: perhaps 'altar' should be read; cf. 1 Kings
xvi. 32 f. (the words for 'pillar' and 'altar' in Hebrew are
much alike).

28–36. This section is mainly the work of the Deuteronomic compiler; but the middle portion (*vv.* 32, 33) is probably
derived from the state annals of the kingdom. In the introduction (*vv.* 28–31) the usual chronological details are not
given; we should also expect a concluding notice of the reign
of Jehoram. Possibly these have been omitted in order to
bring the account of Jehu's reign into immediate connexion with
the story of the reformation ending at *v.* 27.

X. 28–36. THE REIGN OF JEHU.

x. 28–31. *Introduction.*

28
29 Thus Jehu destroyed Baal out of Israel. Howbeit from
the sins of Jeroboam the son of Nebat, wherewith he
made Israel to sin, Jehu departed not from after them,
to wit, the golden calves that were in Beth-el, and that
30 were in Dan. And the LORD said unto Jehu, Because
thou hast done well in executing that which is right in
mine eyes, *and* hast done unto the house of Ahab according to all that was in mine heart, thy sons of the
31 fourth generation shall sit on the throne of Israel. But
Jehu took no heed to walk in the law of the LORD, the
God of Israel, with all his heart: he departed not from
the sins of Jeroboam, wherewith he made Israel to sin.

x. 32, 33. *Hazael's wars against Israel.*

32 In those days the LORD began to cut Israel short: and
33 Hazael smote them in all the coasts of Israel; from
Jordan eastward, all the land of Gilead, the Gadites, and

---

28.   **Thus**: render 'and.'

29.   Jehu maintained the state (Jehovah) worship which had
been established at Dan and Bethel; cf. 1 Kings xii. 28 f., xv.
26, 30, 34.

30.   **thy sons...fourth generation**: cf. xv. 12.

32.   **to cut Israel short**: the expression is peculiar (cf. however, Hab. ii. 10, 'cutting off many peoples'): the Targum
reads 'to be angry with,' and this may be right.

and Hazael smote them etc.: Jehu, as we learn from the
Assyrian inscriptions (cf. note on ix. 2), was a vassal of Assyria
in 842, and, as such, would incur the hostility of Syria, which
had to bear more than one attack from Assyria. With the
cessation of these attacks (after 839) Hazael was able to turn
his attention to his less formidable western neighbour.

33.   **from Jordan eastward**: this clause should be connected
with what precedes; read 'in the whole border of Israel from
Jordan eastward': the whole of the Israelite territory east of
the Jordan, i.e. the land of Gilead (the territory of Reuben,
Gad and the half-tribe of Manasseh) was ravaged by Hazael.

the Reubenites, and the Manassites, from Aroer, which is by the valley of Arnon, even Gilead and Bashan.   Now 34 the rest of the acts of Jehu, and all that he did, and all his might, are they not written in the book of the chronicles of the kings of Israel?   And Jehu slept with 35 his fathers : and they buried him in Samaria.   And Jehoahaz his son reigned in his stead.   And the time 36 that Jehu reigned over Israel in Samaria was twenty and eight years.

XI. 1-20.   ATHALIAH OF JUDAH (cf. 2 Chron. xxii. 10-xxiii. 21).

xi. 1-3.   *Athaliah usurps the throne.*

Now when Athaliah the mother of Ahaziah saw that 11 her son was dead, she arose and destroyed all the seed royal.   But Jehosheba, the daughter of king Joram, sister 2 of Ahaziah, took Joash the son of Ahaziah, and stole him away from among the king's sons that were slain, even him and his nurse, *and put them* in the bedchamber ; and

---

Aroer, the modern *Ar‘air*, lies on a hill on the northern side of the Arnon.   On its site is a heap of ruins.   The severities of Hazael in this war are denounced in Amos i. 3 f. ; cf. 2 Kings viii. 12.

34.   all his might : the LXX (Luc.) adds 'and his conspiracy which he conspired.'

xi. 1 f.   The religious conflict is now transferred to Judah. The worship of the Tyrian Baal, which had been introduced into Jerusalem (cf. xi. 18), and was maintained there for the six years of her reign by Athaliah, the sole survivor of the house of Ahab, is overthrown by a revolution, the promoters of which are not the prophets, but the Temple priesthood.

The narrative in its present form is composite in character (e.g. it gives a double account of Athaliah's death) ; it apparently consists of two originally distinct accounts, one of which is contained in *vv.* 13-18 *a*, and the other in *vv.* 5-12 and 18 *b*.

2.   Jehosheba was the wife of Jehoiada the priest, according to 2 Chron. xxii. 11.

even him and his nurse : these words are probably a gloss ; without them the sentence reads 'from among the king's sons that were to be slain in the bedchamber.'

3 they hid him from Athaliah, so that he was not slain. And
  he was with her hid in the house of the LORD six years:
  and Athaliah reigned over the land.

xi. 4–20. *Joash proclaimed king: the death of Athaliah.*

4   And in the seventh year Jehoiada sent and fetched the
  captains over hundreds, of the Carites and of the guard,
  and brought them to him into the house of the LORD;
  and he made a covenant with them, and took an oath of
  them in the house of the LORD, and shewed them the
5 king's son. And he commanded them, saying, This is

---

3. with her: the Chronicler has 'with them,' i.e. with
Jehoiada and his wife (Jehosheba).

hid in the house etc.: i.e. in one of the residences of the
priests in the Temple; such existed within the old Temple
precincts, apparently.

4–20. In this section the two originally independent accounts
have been amalgamated. It will be noticed that in the principal
narrative (*vv.* 4–12, 18 *b*–20) the *political* side of the revolution
is emphasized, while in the second narrative (*vv.* 13–18 *a*) the
religious and popular side of the movement is dwelt upon. The
two accounts supplement each other.

4. the Carites or 'Carians': the name only occurs here and
in *v.* 19, and denotes mercenaries of some foreign race (like
the *Kĕrēthi* and *Pĕlēthi* [Cherethites and Pelethites]) employed
in the royal body-guard; cf. 1 Kings i. 38; 2 Sam. viii. 18,
xv. 18, xx. 7, 23. Possibly 'Carians' here is a scribal error for
'Cherethites.' These foreign troops, it is to be noticed, guard
the Temple. In the Chronicler's account their place is taken
by Levites.

took an oath...house of the Lord: or rather 'made them
swear by the house of Jehovah'; cf. Matt. xxiii. 16.

5–8. The interpretation of the directions given to the cen-
turions in these verses is complicated by our ignorance of the
ordinary arrangements followed in the disposition of the guards.
What appears to be the best explanation is as follows. The
guard was divided into three companies, two of which were on
duty on week-days in the palace, and one in the Temple. On
Sabbaths the order was reversed; two companies were in the
Temple, and one in the palace, the palace-guard (of two companies) marching to the Temple to relieve the one company on
guard there. Jehoiada's plan is to assemble all three companies
at a given time in the Temple, and leave the palace entirely

the thing that ye shall do: a third part of you, that come in on the sabbath, shall be keepers of the watch of the king's house; and a third part shall be at the gate Sur; 6 and a third part at the gate behind the guard: so shall ye keep the watch of the house, and be a barrier. And 7 the two companies of you, even all that go forth on the sabbath, shall keep the watch of the house of the LORD about the king. And ye shall compass the king round 8 about, every man with his weapons in his hand; and he that cometh within the ranks, let him be slain: and be ye with the 'king when he goeth out, and when he cometh in. And the captains over hundreds did according to 9 all that Jehoiada the priest commanded: and they took every man his men, those that were to come in on the sabbath, with those that were to go out on the sabbath, and came to Jehoiada the priest. And the priest delivered 10

---

denuded of troops. For this purpose the time selected is the moment on the Sabbath when the two companies have arrived from the palace to relieve the third company on duty in the Temple. This third company is detained, and so the whole body of troops is assembled, and the king is proclaimed. It should be remembered that the troops who went back to the palace would go into their quarters, and, for the most part, be relieved of duty. On this view of the text *v.* 6 must be regarded as a gloss. The directions (with some slight emendation) will now run as follows: 'the third part of you, those that come in (turn in) on the Sabbath (i.e. those that return to the palace), and keep the watch of the king's house (*v.* 5); and the two (other) companies of you—even all that go forth (i.e. turn out from the barracks in the palace) on the Sabbath, and keep the watch of the house of the Lord (*v.* 7: omit 'about the king' at the end of the verse): ye shall compass the king round about' etc. (*v.* 8).

6. at the gate Sur: the 'gate of Sur' (*Sur* = 'turning aside') may have been a side exit from the court of the palace (Ball); or (with a slight change) 'horse-gate' (cf. *v.* 16) can be read. The whole verse is probably an incorrect gloss.

8. when he goeth out etc.: i.e. the whole guard was to surround the king when he went out (from the Temple), and when he came in (to the palace). Nobody was to be allowed to break 'within the ranks' to approach the king.

to the captains over hundreds the spears and shields that
had been king David's, which were in the house of the
11 LORD.   And the guard stood, every man with his weapons
in his hand, from the right side of the house to the left
side of the house, along by the altar and the house, by
12 the king round about.   Then he brought out the king's
son, and put the crown upon him, and *gave him* the
testimony; and they made him king, and anointed him;
and they clapped their hands, and said, God save the
13 king.   And when Athaliah heard the noise of the guard
and of the people, she came to the people intò the house
14 of the LORD: and she looked, and, behold, the king
stood by the pillar, as the manner was, and the captains
and the trumpets by the king; and all the people of the
land rejoiced, and blew with trumpets.   Then Athaliah
15 rent her clothes, and cried, Treason, treason.   And

---

10.   the spears and shields etc.: David's own 'spears and
shields' may have been preserved in the Temple, and used
ceremonially in coronations.   It is not to be supposed that the
troops were unarmed, and that weapons were distributed to
them from the Temple armoury.   Some scholars think the words
are a gloss (from 2 Chronicles).

11.   from the right side etc.: i.e. the troops were drawn up
right across the Temple-court, from north to south, and facing
the altar.

by the king round about: since the king had not yet appeared the words must be an incorrect gloss.

12.   the testimony: i.e. the law-book.   But the context de-
mands something connected with the regalia.   Qimḥi explains
the expression to mean a royal robe.   Perhaps (by a probable
emendation) 'the bracelets' (cf. 2 Sam. i. 10) should be read.

13.   Here begins the second narrative, in which the people
under its military leaders plays the prominent part.

of the guard *and of* **the people**: the words 'of the guard
and' should probably be omitted as a harmonizing gloss.

14.   by the pillar: or rather 'on the stand,' probably a dais
where it was customary for the king to stand when he was
present at the Temple-worship.   According to 2 Chron. xxiii.
13 it was placed before the great altar at the entrance to the
inner court.

Jehoiada the priest commanded the captains of hundreds
that were set over the host, and said unto them, Have
her forth between the ranks; and him that followeth her
slay with the sword: for the priest said, Let her not be
slain in the house of the LORD. So they made way for 16
her; and she went by the way of the horses' entry to the
king's house: and there was she slain.

And Jehoiada made a covenant between the LORD 17
and the king and the people, that they should be the
LORD'S people; between the king also and the people.
And all the people of the land went to the house of Baal, 18
and brake it down; his altars and his images brake they
in pieces thoroughly, and slew Mattan the priest of Baal
before the altars. And the priest appointed officers over
the house of the LORD. And he took the captains over 19

---

15. the captains of hundreds: omit these words as probably a gloss (from *vv.* 4, 9, 10). The words immediately following should be read 'the commanders of the army.'
   between the ranks may also be a later addition to the text.
   16. they made way for her: better 'they laid hands on
her.'
   the horses' entry may be identical with the gate mentioned
in *v.* 6 (emended text). Another gate is mentioned in *v.* 19.
Athaliah was conducted to the palace stables and there put to
death.
   17. a covenant: the Heb. has 'the covenant': the covenant
which is renewed has a double aspect; on the one hand it
renews the religious bond between Jehovah and king and people,
which had been violated by the tolerance of Baal-worship; the
nation again becomes 'the people of Jehovah': on the other
hand it re-establishes proper relations between the king and the
people.
   18. And all the people...altars: the revolution culminates,
according to the second account which ends here, in the extirpation of the Baal-worship in Jerusalem.
   Mattan, a contraction of *Mattan-baal* ('gift of Baal'), a name
of frequent occurrence in Phoenician inscriptions.
   And the priest etc.: these words form the immediate continuation of *v.* 12 (first account): **officers** should rather be
guard or **watches**.
   19. The king is now solemnly escorted to the palace by

hundreds, and the Carites, and the guard, and all the
people of the land ; and they brought down the king
from the house of the LORD, and came by the way of
the gate of the guard unto the king's house. And he
20 sat on the throne of the kings. So all the people of the
land rejoiced, and the city was quiet : and they slew
Athaliah with the sword at the king's house.

XI. 21–XII. 21. JEHOASH OF JUDAH (cf. 2 Chron. xxiv.).

xi. 21, xii. 1-3. *Introduction.*

21 Jehoash was seven years old when he began to reign.
12 In the seventh year of Jehu began Jehoash to reign ; and
he reigned forty years in Jerusalem : and his mother's
2 name was Zibiah of Beer-sheba. And Jehoash did that
which was right in the eyes of the LORD all his days
3 wherein Jehoiada the priest instructed him. Howbeit
the high places were not taken away : the people still
sacrificed and burnt incense in the high places.

---

priests, guards, and people, and there enthroned (cf. 1 Kings i.
35, 46).

20. the city was quiet: no opposition was raised.

and they slew Athaliah: this event has already been once
described (in the first account) ; cf. *v.* 16.

21 f. In the Hebrew Bible the division of the chapters is
correct ; thus xi. 21–xii. 21 (E.V.) = xii. 1-22 in the Hebrew.
The opening clauses have become displaced ; read, with LXX
(Luc.), 'In the seventh year of Jehu began Jehoash to reign ;
Jehoash was seven years old when he began to reign.' This is
the usual order.

xii. 1. In the seventh year: cf. xi. 4. Consequently Jehoash,
at the time when Athaliah seized the throne, was less than one
year old.

2. all his days wherein etc.: render, rather, 'all his days,
forasmuch as' etc. The writer means that Jehoash was a pious
king the whole of his reign, the benefit of his early instruction
by Jehoiada lasting to the end. The Chronicler (2 Chron. xxiv.
2) modifies this estimate.

xii. 4–16. *Regulations regarding the repair of the Temple-fabric.*

And Jehoash said to the priests, All the money of the 4 hallowed things that is brought into the house of the LORD, in current money, the money of the persons for whom each man is rated, and all the money that it cometh into any man's heart to bring into the house of the LORD, let the priests take it to them, every man from 5 his acquaintance: and they shall repair the breaches of the house, wheresoever any breach shall be found. But 6 it was so, that in the three and twentieth year of king Jehoash the priests had not repaired the breaches of the

---

4–16. The regulations set forth in this section appear to have continued in force up to the time of the Exile (cf. ch. xxii.). Till the time of Jehoash the expense of maintaining the Temple-fabric seems to have been a charge on the royal revenues. Now the priests were entrusted with the collection of the Temple-dues, and were made responsible for the repairs. But this plan not proving satisfactory, another was later adopted. The dues were collected by a royal official and paid over directly to those responsible for the work. It is probable that the source from which this section was derived was not the royal annals, from which the compiler draws the political material for his history, but a Temple-history which has been utilized in other parts of 1 and 2 Kings (1 Kings vi., vii.; 2 Kings xxii., xxiii., and possibly xi. 5–12, 18 *b*–20, xvi. 10 f.).

4. **All the money** etc.: the Temple-revenues are derived from two classes of payments, one fixed by a tariff, the other from free-will offerings. Both are the subject of this verse.

in current money etc.: this clause is difficult; 'current money' must mean money (silver) in bars or ingots of a certain weight (cf. Gen. xxiii. 16). The LXX (Luc.) gives a different text. Following this we may read 'the money of each man's assess-ment' (cf. Lev. xxvii. 2 f.), omitting 'the money of the persons for whom each man is rated,' which probably represents a doublet.

and all the money etc.: i.e. from free-will offerings.

5. **acquaintance**: i.e. persons resorting to the Temple to make offerings would deal with a priest personally known to them. In the case of private offerings this might be customary. But the word rendered 'acquaintance' is of doubtful meaning, and occurs only here and in *v.* 8.

7 house. Then king Jehoash called for Jehoiada the priest, and for the *other* priests, and said unto them, Why repair ye not the breaches of the house? now therefore take no *more* money from your acquaintance, but deliver it for 8 the breaches of the house. And the priests consented that they should take no *more* money from the people, 9 neither repair the breaches of the house. But Jehoiada the priest took a chest, and bored a hole in the lid of it, and set it beside the altar, on the right side as one cometh into the house of the LORD: and the priests that kept the door put therein all the money that was brought into the 10 house of the LORD. And it was so, when they saw that there was much money in the chest, that the king's scribe and the high priest came up, and they put up in bags and told the money that was found in the house of the 11 LORD. And they gave the money that was weighed out into the hands of them that did the work, that had the oversight of the house of the LORD: and they paid it out to the carpenters and the builders, that wrought upon 12 the house of the LORD, and to the masons and the hewers of stone, and for buying timber and hewn stone

---

7. Then king Jehoash etc.: it is to be noticed that the king takes the initiative. The sanctuary is really under his control. The Temple was still essentially the royal chapel.

9. beside the altar etc.: the altar stood in the midst of the court, but the money was received by the priests 'that kept the threshold' (margin), i.e. from persons as they entered the sanctuary. Probably some other word should be read, perhaps 'beside the doorpost.' Another suggestion is 'beside the pillar' (*masseba*) of which there were more than one in the Temple (cf. xviii. 4, xxiii. 4 f.); but this is less likely, as the 'pillars' would probably be within the Temple.

kept the door: or rather 'threshold,' an important office; cf. xxii. 4, xxiii. 4, xxv. 18; Jer. xxxv. 4.

10. and the high priest: elsewhere in the narrative Jehoiada is simply called 'the priest,' and it is doubtful whether the title 'high priest,' as here used, can be anywhere authentically attested in pre-exilic writings. Not improbably it is an addition here to the original account.

to repair the breaches of the house of the LORD, and for
all that was laid out for the house to repair it. But there 13
were not made for the house of the LORD cups of silver,
snuffers, basons, trumpets, any vessels of gold, or vessels
of silver, of the money that was brought into the house
of the LORD: for they gave that to them that did the 14
work, and repaired therewith the house of the LORD.
Moreover they reckoned not with the men, into whose 15
hand they delivered the money to give to them that did the
work: for they dealt faithfully. The money for the guilt 16
offerings, and the money for the sin offerings, was not
brought into the house of the LORD: it was the priests'.

xii. 17, 18. *Hazael spares Jerusalem.*

Then Hazael king of Syria went up, and fought against 17
Gath, and took it: and Hazael set his face to go up to

---

13. cups of silver etc.: cf. 1 Kings vii. 50. All the money
was required for the work of structural renovation.

15. they dealt faithfully: i.e. the officials who superintended
the work, and who received the money and paid the workmen,
could be trusted absolutely; it was unnecessary to 'reckon'
with them the sums handed over.

16. The priests retained the revenue derived from two
sources, viz. **money for the guilt offerings** and **money for the
sin offerings**. In both cases money fines are referred to for
offences, which in later times were atoned for by special kinds
of sacrifice (cf. Lev. iv., v.).

17, 18. It is clear from this short notice that Hazael carried
his successful wars with Israel (cf. x. 32, xiii. 3) into the south.
In one of these campaigns he captured Gath, which seems to
have been a dependency of Judah, and so was able to threaten
Jerusalem, which was only spared after the Temple had been
stripped of its treasures. The reference to the Temple suggests
that the source may have been the Temple-history (cf. note on
vv. 4–16 above), though most scholars think the Judaean royal
annals have here been utilized by the compiler.

17. Gath was one of the five principal cities of the Philistines,
and lay between Ekron and Ashdod: but the exact site is uncertain. It was an important stronghold covering the approach
to Jerusalem on the west.

18 Jerusalem.   And Jehoash king of Judah took all the
hallowed things that Jehoshaphat, and Jehoram, and
Ahaziah, his fathers, kings of Judah, had dedicated, and
his own hallowed things, and all the gold that was found
in the treasures of the house of the LORD, and of the
king's house, and sent it to Hazael king of Syria : and
he went away from Jerusalem.

xii. 19, 20.   Conclusion.

19 Now the rest of the acts of Joash, and all that he did,
are they not written in the book of the chronicles of the
20 kings of Judah? And his servants arose, and made a
conspiracy, and smote Joash at the house of Millo, *on*
21 *the way* that goeth down to Silla.   For Jozacar the son
of Shimeath, and Jehozabad the son of Shomer, his
servants, smote him, and he died; and they buried him
with his fathers in the city of David : and Amaziah his
son reigned in his stead.

XIII. 1-9.   JEHOAHAZ OF ISRAEL.
xiii. 1, 2.   Introduction.

13   In the three and twentieth year of Joash the son of
Ahaziah, king of Judah, Jehoahaz the son of Jehu began

---

18.   the hallowed things etc.: for other occasions when the
Temple was stripped of treasure for foreign tribute, cf. 1 Kings
xv. 18 (Asa); 2 Kings xvi. 17, 18 (Ahaz), xviii. 16 (Hezekiah).
The kings seem to have regarded the Temple-treasures as royal
property.

20.   the house of Millo...Silla: 'house of Millo,' or rather
'*Beth Millo*' is apparently the name of a locality otherwise
unknown.   It is not clear that it had any connexion with 'the
Millo' of 2 Sam. v. 9, 1 Kings ix. 15 etc., which was the
name of a part of the fortifications of the city of David.   'Silla'
is probably corrupt, and may be merely a variant of *Millo*.

21.   smote him etc.: both Jehoash and his son Amaziah were
assassinated.   No reason is here given ; probably it was an act
of private vengeance, perhaps, as the Chronicler relates, for
the execution of Zechariah the son of Jehoiada (cf. 2 Chron.
xxiv. 25-26).

xiii. 1-9.   In this section *vv.* 4-6 are a difficulty.   According
to *v.* 3 the Syrian oppression lasted during the entire reign of

to reign over Israel in Samaria, *and reigned* seventeen
years.   And he did that which was evil in the sight of 2
the LORD, and followed the sins of Jeroboam the son of
Nebat, wherewith he made Israel to sin ; he departed
not therefrom.

xiii. 3-7.   *The Syrian oppression.*

And the anger of the LORD was kindled against Israel, 3
and he delivered them into the hand of Hazael king
of Syria, and into the hand of Ben-hadad the son of
Hazael, continually.   And Jehoahaz besought the LORD, 4
and the LORD hearkened unto him: for he saw the
oppression of Israel, how that the king of Syria oppressed them.   (And the LORD gave Israel a saviour, 5
so that they went out from under the hand of the
Syrians : and the children of Israel dwelt in their tents,
as beforetime.   Nevertheless they departed not from the 6
sins of the house of Jeroboam, wherewith he made Israel
to sin, but walked therein : and there remained the
Asherah also in Samaria.)   For he left not to Jehoahaz 7

Jehoahaz; but *vv.* 3-6 modify this statement and say that after
Jehoahaz had besought the Lord deliverance was granted.   The
verses appear to be an insertion by a later hand, and can only
apply to the time of Joash (and later), when the tide of Syrian
conquest began to turn (cf. *vv.* 15 f.).   Possibly xiii. 23 and xiv.
26 f. are examples of similar interpolation by a later scribe.

3. continually: i.e. without a break.

4. besought the Lord: cf. 1 Kings xiii. 6 (the same phrase).

5. a saviour: or 'deliverer' (cf. Judges iii. 9, 15).   The
'deliverer' was Jeroboam II, the grandson of Jehoahaz; cf. xiv.
27.   Some scholars have supposed that the Assyrians (whose
movement westward had begun to pre-occupy Syria) are intended.

6. the Asherah: i.e. the emblem (pole or tree-trunk) of the
sacred tree, erected by the side of the altar.   Whether this
emblem had any connexion with the worship of a goddess, who
is herself sometimes called *Asherah* (cf. 1 Kings xv. 13 ; 2 Kings
xxi. 7, xxiii. 4 ; and see also Judges vi. 26; Deut. xvi. 21; Jer.
xvii. 2), is uncertain.   Some scholars deny the existence of such
a goddess.

7. For he left not etc.: i.e. Jehovah probably (not Hazael)

of the people save fifty horsemen, and ten chariots, and
ten thousand footmen ; for the king of Syria destroyed
them, and made them like the dust in threshing.

xiii. 8, 9. *Conclusion.*

8 Now the rest of the acts of Jehoahaz, and all that he did,
and his might, are they not written in the book of the
9 chronicles of the kings of Israel? And Jehoahaz slept
with his fathers ; and they buried him in Samaria : and
Joash his son reigned in his stead.

XIII. 10-25. JEHOASH OF ISRAEL.

xiii. 10, 11. *Introduction.*

10   In the thirty and seventh year of Joash king of Judah
began Jehoash the son of Jehoahaz to reign over Israel
11 in Samaria, *and reigned* sixteen years. And he did that
which was evil in the sight of the LORD; he departed
not from all the sins of Jeroboam the son of Nebat,
wherewith he made Israel to sin : but he walked therein.

---

did not leave. This verse forms the immediate continuation of
v. 3. The brackets which in the R.V. enclose *vv.* 5, 6 should
rather include *vv.* 4–6, the whole forming a parenthesis.

of the people: i.e. of the male population capable of bearing
arms. This indicates how serious the losses caused by the war
had been.

10-25. This section has some remarkable features : the concluding formula (*vv.* 12, 13) immediately follows the introductory
notice (*vv.* 10, 11), and is succeeded by a section containing the
conclusion of the Elisha-narratives (*vv.* 14–21), and another
extracted from the Israelite annals (*vv.* 22–25). The most
probable solution of the difficulties of the section appears to
be the following. Originally xiv. 8–16, which contains the
concluding formula for the reign of Jehoash, followed xiii. 25,
but was later transferred, for some reason, to its present position,
together with the concluding verses about Jehoash (xiv. 15, 16).
This procedure left our present section without a conclusion,
which was made good by a later hand by the insertion of
vv. 12, 13.

10. the thirty and seventh year: probably an error for
'the thirty-ninth year'; cf. xiii. 1 and xiv. 1.

xiii. 12, 13.   *Conclusion.*

Now the rest of the acts of Joash, and all that he did, 12
and his might wherewith he fought against Amaziah
king of Judah, are they not written in the book of the
chronicles of the kings of Israel? And Joash slept 13
with his fathers; and Jeroboam sat upon his throne:
and Joash was buried in Samaria with the kings of
Israel.

xiii. 14–21.   *Elisha's death and burial.*

Now Elisha was fallen sick of his sickness whereof 14
he died: and Joash the king of Israel came down unto
him, and wept over him, and said, My father, my father,
the chariots of Israel and the horsemen thereof! And 15
Elisha said unto him, Take bow and arrows: and he
took unto him bow and arrows. And he said to the 16
king of Israel, Put thine hand upon the bow: and he put
his hand *upon it.* And Elisha laid his hands upon the
king's hands. And he said, Open the window eastward: 17
and he opened it. Then Elisha said, Shoot: and he shot.
And he said, The LORD'S arrow of victory, even the arrow

12, 13. These verses were probably inserted by a later hand
(see above); cf. xiv. 15, 16.

14–21.   This section forms the conclusion of the Elisha-cycle
of biographical narratives, and was extracted from the same
source.   Its insertion here is due to the fact that it records an
incident in which Jehoash was concerned.   The aged prophet
displays a pathetic loyalty to the dynasty of Jehu which he had
helped to establish.

14.   whereof he died : or better 'was to die.'

over him : 'over his face' (margin), i.e. as he lay upon his
bed.

My father etc.: cf. vi. 21 and ii. 12.   Elisha had been more
to Israel than armies of chariots and horsemen.

17.   eastward : i.e. in the direction of Damascus.   To shoot
an arrow into the enemy's country was an old symbolical way
of declaring war; cf. Virgil, *Aen.* IX. 57.

of victory over Syria: for thou shalt smite the Syrians in
18 Aphek, till thou have consumed them.   And he said, Take
the arrows: and he took them.   And he said unto the king
of Israel, Smite upon the ground: and he smote thrice,
19 and stayed.   And the man of God was wroth with him,
and said, Thou shouldest have smitten five or six times;
then hadst thou smitten Syria till thou hadst consumed
it: whereas now thou shalt smite Syria but thrice.
20   And Elisha died, and they buried him.   Now the
bands of the Moabites invaded the land at the coming
21 in of the year.   And it came to pass, as they were burying
a man, that, behold, they spied a band; and they cast
the man into the sepulchre of Elisha: and as soon as
the man touched the bones of Elisha, he revived, and
stood up on his feet.

---

in Aphek: Aphek here is probably identical with the Aphek
mentioned in 1 Sam. xxix. 1, and if so was situated not far from
Jezreel.   It served as a base for the Syrian attacks on Israel
(cf. 1 Kings xx. 26).   The promise refers to fighting, the
details of which are not recorded.

18.   he smote thrice, and stayed: divination by arrows like
the casting of lots was a common practice among the ancient
Semites.   Here the method is adopted, with the sanction of the
prophet, as a means of ascertaining the divine will, on the
principle expressed in Prov. xvi. 33 ('The lot is cast into the
lap, but the whole disposing thereof is of the Lord').   The king's
lack of zeal in only smiting three times aroused the prophet's
anger, suggesting, as it does, a similar inability to prosecute the
war with determination.

20.   invaded: rather 'used to invade.'

at the coming in of the year: read, probably, 'year by year.'

21.   sepulchre of Elisha: the LXX (Luc.) adds 'and went
away.'

22–25.   The death of Hazael was followed by the partial
recovery of Israel.   The main contributory cause, however,
seems to have been the renewal of Assyrian activity in the west.
About 803 B.C. the Assyrian king Ramman-nirari III made an
expedition to the Mediterranean coast, subduing Damascus on
the way.   The source of the passage was probably the Israelitish
annalistic document, though v. 23 appears to be an interpolation
by a later hand, of the same character as vv. 4–6.

xiii. 22-25. *Israelite successes against Syria.*

And Hazael king of Syria oppressed Israel all the days 22 of Jehoahaz. But the LORD was gracious unto them, 23 and had compassion on them, and had respect unto them, because of his covenant with Abraham, Isaac, and Jacob, and would not destroy them, neither cast he them from his presence as yet. And Hazael king of Syria 24 died; and Ben-hadad his son reigned in his stead. And 25 Jehoash the son of Jehoahaz took again out of the hand of Ben-hadad the son of Hazael the cities which he had taken out of the hand of Jehoahaz his father by war. Three times did Joash smite him, and recovered the cities of Israel.

XIV. 1-22. AMAZIAH OF JUDAH (cf. 2 Chron. xxv.).

xiv. 1-4. *Introduction.*

In the second year of Joash son of Joahaz king of 14 Israel began Amaziah the son of Joash king of Judah to reign. He was twenty and five years old when he began 2 to reign; and he reigned twenty and nine years in

---

22. oppressed: rather 'had oppressed.' At the end of this verse the LXX (Luc.) adds a notice which is probably original : 'and Hazael had taken the Philistines out of his (Jehoahaz's) hand from the western sea unto Aphek.' This may refer to the campaign alluded to in xii. 18.

23. With this verse cf. *vv.* 4-6 (probably by the same hand).

24. Ben-hadad his son: the king mentioned on the Assyrian inscription by Ramman-nirari is *Mari*, and is probably identical with Ben-hadad here. Three kings of the name are mentioned in the O.T. (1 Kings xv. 18, xx. 1 and this passage).

25. the cities etc.: the cities meant must have been on the west side of the Jordan, and probably included Lo-debar and Karnaim, according to Amos vi. 13 (emended text).

xiv. 1-4. The introductory section (*vv.* 1-4) together with *vv.* 5, 6, and the greater part of the concluding section (*vv.* 17-22) are the work of the Deuteronomic compiler. The intervening sections are drawn from other sources.

2. twenty and nine years: from a comparison with xiii. 10 and xv. 1 it is clear that a serious error (amounting to over

Jerusalem : and his mother's name was Jehoaddin of
3 Jerusalem.   And he did that which was right in the eyes
of the LORD, yet not like David his father : he did ac-
4 cording to all that Joash his father had done.   Howbeit
the high places were not taken away : the people still
sacrificed and burnt incense in the high places.

xiv. 5, 6.   *Execution of the assassins of Jehoash.*

5 And it came to pass, as soon as the kingdom was established in his hand, that he slew his servants which had
6 slain the king his father : but the children of the murderers
he put not to death : according to that which is written
in the book of the law of Moses, as the LORD commanded, saying, The fathers shall not be put to death
for the children, nor the children be put to death for the
fathers ; but every man shall die for his own sin.

xiv. 7.   *War with Edom.*

7 He slew of Edom in the Valley of Salt ten thousand, and

---

twenty years) has been made in the chronological scheme : cf.
xv. 8 and note, and see further *Introduction*, § 4 (possibly the
reign should be reduced to nine years).

4.   burnt incense : or rather ' offered by burning ' ; cf. xvii. 5.
the high places etc. : cf. 1 Kings iii. 2 f.

5.   his servants etc. : cf. xii. 20, 21.

6.   the children etc. : the special mention of the sparing of
the murderers' children seems to indicate that such was an
innovation.   The reference to **the book of the law of Moses**
is an allusion to Deut. xxiv. 16 (the Deuteronomic law-book
was the only ' law of Moses ' known to the compiler).   For the
older practice (of slaughtering the children of condemned persons)
cf. Joshua vii. 24 f.

7.   Edom had maintained its independence : no attempt to
subdue it had been made since Jehoram's unsuccessful expedition (cf. viii. 20-22).   The source of this passage was probably
the Judaean annalistic document.

the Valley of Salt is usually regarded as a name for the marshy
plain south of the Dead Sea (cf. 2 Sam. viii. 13).

took Sela by war, and called the name of it Joktheel,
unto this day.

xiv. 8–14 (15, 16). *War between Judah and Israel.*

Then Amaziah sent messengers to Jehoash, the son of 8
Jehoahaz son of Jehu, king of Israel, saying, Come, let
us look one another in the face. And Jehoash the king 9
of Israel sent to Amaziah king of Judah, saying, The
thistle that was in Lebanon sent to the cedar that was in
Lebanon, saying, Give thy daughter to my son to wife:
and there passed by a wild beast that was in Lebanon,
and trode down the thistle. Thou hast indeed smitten 10
Edom, and thine heart hath lifted thee up: glory thereof,
and abide at home; for why shouldest thou meddle to

Sela (margin 'the rock'): the usual identification of Sela with
Petra ('the rock city'), the capital of Edom, has been disputed.

Joktheel: a Judaean town bore this name; cf. Josh. xv. 38.
Amaziah's victory over Edom did not, apparently, result in its
permanent subjugation by Judah at this time.

8–14. The tone of the section suggests that it was derived
from a north-Israelitish source (but not the Israelitish annals);
notice especially the contemptuous way in which Judah and its
king are referred to. It is hardly probable that Judah continued to be a vassal-state to north Israel after the extinction of
Omri's dynasty; but it was still markedly inferior in power and
resources to the northern kingdom. Amaziah's rash challenge
can only be explained by his recent success over Edom. The
original position of this section was probably immediately after
xiii. 25; when it is restored to its proper position, *vv.* 15, 16 form
the appropriate conclusion to the reign of Jehoash of Israel (see
the notes above on xiii. 10, 11).

8. look another in the face: perhaps this is a mere
assertion of a claim to treat with the Israelite king on terms
of equality, and no longer (as in the past) as an inferior.
Some commentators regard it as a challenge to battle.

9. The thistle...cedar: the parable of the thistle (or bramble)
and the cedar points the contrast between the northern and
southern kingdoms as regards relative power and importance;
cf. Jotham's parable (Judges ix. 7 f.).

Give thy daughter etc.: Jehoash, apparently, understands
Amaziah's demand to be one for alliance on equal terms.

10. meddle to *thy* **hurt:** or rather, as margin, 'provoke
calamity.'

thy hurt, that thou shouldest fall, even thou, and Judah
11 with thee? But Amaziah would not hear. So Jehoash
king of Israel went up; and he and Amaziah king of
Judah looked one another in the face at Beth-shemesh,
12 which belongeth to Judah. And Judah was put to the
worse before Israel; and they fled every man to his tent.
13 And Jehoash king of Israel took Amaziah king of Judah,
the son of Jehoash the son of Ahaziah, at Beth-shemesh,
and came to Jerusalem, and brake down the wall of
Jerusalem from the gate of Ephraim unto the corner
14 gate, four hundred cubits. And he took all the gold and
silver, and all the vessels that were found in the house
of the LORD, and in the treasures of the king's house,
15 the hostages also, and returned to Samaria. Now the
rest of the acts of Jehoash which he did, and his might,
and how he fought with Amaziah king of Judah, are they
not written in the book of the chronicles of the kings of
16 Israel? And Jehoash slept with his fathers, and was
buried in Samaria with the kings of Israel; and Jeroboam
his son reigned in his stead.

xiv. 17–22. *Conclusion.*

17   And Amaziah the son of Joash king of Judah lived
after the death of Jehoash son of Jehoahaz king of Israel

---

11. Beth-shemesh etc.: Beth-shemesh is the modern '*Ain
shems*, a village about four miles from Jerusalem on one of the
roads to Joppa. The addition of **which belongeth to Judah**
betrays the hand of a north-Israelitish writer (cf. 1 Kings xix. 3).
    13. and came: read 'and brought him' (so LXX, and
2 Chron. xxv. 23).
    brake down the wall...corner gate: the 'gate of Ephraim,'
as the name suggests, must have been that which opened on the
road to the north (to Ephraim), and **the corner gate** was probably the name of the gate at the north-west angle of the wall.
By the demolition of a considerable part of the northern wall
of the city it was made plain that Jerusalem was no longer
independent of north Israel, but free and open to the north.
    four hundred cubits: if we reckon the cubit as = 20 inches,
the distance would be over 220 yards.

fifteen years.   Now the rest of the acts of Amaziah, are 18
they not written in the book of the chronicles of the
kings of Judah?   And they made a conspiracy against 19
him in Jerusalem ; and he fled to Lachish : but they sent
after him to Lachish, and slew him there.   And they 20
brought him upon horses : and he was buried at Jerusalem with his fathers in the city of David.   And all the 21
people of Judah took Azariah, who was sixteen years old,
and made him king in the room of his father Amaziah.
He built Elath, and restored it to Judah, after that the 22
king slept with his fathers.

17–22.   In this section *v.* 17 is apparently a later insertion
suggested by the displacement of *vv.* 15, 16.   It was felt to be
necessary to define the interval that elapsed between the death
of Jehoash of Israel (*v.* 16) and the end of Amaziah's reign.   In
vv. 19–22 the compiler has probably utilized annalistic material.

17.   fifteen years : according to the chronology of xiii. 10,
xiv. 2.

19.   a conspiracy : in this case a popular uprising brought
about, probably, by the unfortunate results of Amaziah's reckless
policy.   It was not directed against the dynasty.

Lachish : about 35 miles south-west of Jerusalem, if we accept
the identification of the site by Petrie with *Tell el-Ḥasi.*

22.   Elath : cf. 1 Kings ix. 26.   The town (=the modern
Aḳaba) stood at the head of the gulf named after it (=the Gulf
of Aḳaba).   Its possession was important for commercial purposes.   The position of this notice is peculiar.   It has been
suggested that Amaziah may have captured the port (cf. *v.* 7),
and then lost it, and that one of the first acts of the young
Azariah was to regain possession of it.   But in any case the
more natural position for the verse would be in the formal
account of Azariah's reign.

23–29.   The long and brilliant reign (41 years) of the most
successful of the north-Israelitish kings is dealt with very sum-
marily and baldly in this section.   A truer picture of the pros-
perity—and luxury—of the time can be seen in the writings of
Amos and Hosea.   The compiler may have had access to full
and detailed accounts, which he has preferred to compress.
The territorial expansion of the north-Israelitish kingdom under
Jeroboam II was made possible by the fact that Syria had been
permanently crippled by the Assyrians under Shalmaneser III
(782–772) and his successor, while there was a lull in these

XIV. 23–2'). JEROBOAM II OF ISRAEL.

xiv. 23, 24. *Introduction.*

23 In the fifteenth year of Amaziah the son of Joash king
of Judah Jeroboam the son of Joash king of Israel began
24 to reign in Samaria, *and reigned* forty and one years. And
he did that which was evil in the sight of the LORD : he
departed not from all the sins of Jeroboam the son of
Nebat, wherewith he made Israel to sin.

xiv. 25–27. *Solomon's empire re-established.*

25 He restored the border of Israel from the entering in of
Hamath unto the sea of the Arabah, according to the word
of the LORD, the God of Israel, which he spake by the
hand of his servant Jonah the son of Amittai, the prophet,
26 which was of Gath-hepher. For the LORD saw the afflic-
tion of Israel, that it was very bitter : for there was none
shut up nor left at large, neither was there any helper for

---

activities under the next Assyrian monarch, Asshur-nirari (754–
746 B.C.), which gave Jeroboam an opportunity of which he
made full use. Under Jeroboam the old limits of Solomon's
empire were attained.

23. In the fifteenth year etc.: this chronological statement
agrees with xiv. 1 and 17, but is irreconcileable with xv. 8.
See further *Introduction*, § 4.

25–27. Verses 26, 27 are of the same character as xiii. 4 f.
and 23, and are probably by the same hand.

25. from...Hamath: i.e. from the approach of Hamath
(= the modern *Ḥamā* on the Orontes); this marks the ideal
northern limit of Israel, which was attained only under Solomon
and Jeroboam II; cf. 1 Kings viii. 65. The approach to
Hamath is probably identical with the pass between Hermon
and Lebanon through which entrance to Coele-Syria is gained.

the sea of the Arabah: i.e. the Dead Sea.

Jonah...Gath-hepher: this prophet was probably a contemporary of Elisha ; our present book of Jonah is a later writing
which has taken this prophet as its hero. Gath-hepher lay,
according to Josh. xix. 13, on the eastern border of Zebulon,
and its site is probably not far from Nazareth, in the neighbourhood of which the tomb of the prophet is still shown.

26. shut up etc.: cf. ix. 8 and note.

Israel. And the LORD said not that he would blot out 27
the name of Israel from under heaven: but he saved
them by the hand of Jeroboam the son of Joash.

xiv. 28, 29. *Conclusion.*

Now the rest of the acts of Jeroboam, and all that he 28
did, and his might, how he warred, and how he recovered
Damascus, and Hamath, *which had belonged* to Judah,
for Israel, are they not written in the book of the
chronicles of the kings of Israel? And Jeroboam slept 29
with his fathers, even with the kings of Israel; and
Zechariah his son reigned in his stead.

XV. 1–7. AZARIAH (UZZIAH) OF JUDAH (cf. 2 Chron. xxvi.).

xv. 1–4. *Introduction.*

In the twenty and seventh year of Jeroboam king of 15

---

27. saved them: 'delivered them'; cf. xiii. 5 and note.
28. and how he recovered...**Israel**: the text yields no
tolerable sense, and is certainly corrupt. The R.V. rendering
suggests that Damascus and Hamath had once formed part of
the territory of Judah, for which there is no warrant. Hamath
was never included in David's kingdom (cf. 2 Sam. xiii. 9 f.),
nor would David's empire be designated *Judah*. The Versions
give no help. Burney proposes to emend the text so as to read,
'and how he fought with Damascus and how he turned away
the wrath (Heb. *ḥămath*) of Jehovah from Israel.'
xv. 1–7. Here again the compiler's account of a long and
successful reign is bald and colourless. From the early prophecies of Isaiah it is clear that for a considerable period Judah
under Azariah (Uzziah) prospered exceedingly, and this is confirmed by other allusions in Amos and Hosea. The supposed
reference to Azariah in an inscription of Tiglath-Pileser III as
the leader of a confederacy of Syrian states in 738 B.C. has been
called in question. It is doubtful whether *Ja'udi* there ('Azariah
of Ja'udi) can be identified with Judah. The Chronicler gives
many details of the military successes and able administration of
Azariah (Uzziah).
1. twenty and seventh year: here again the chronology
cannot be reconciled with xiv. 2, 23. If the first year of Jeroboam = the fifteenth year of Amaziah (xiv. 23), and Amaziah
reigned twenty-nine years (xiv. 2, 17), then the first year of
Azariah must = the fifteenth year of Jeroboam. See *Introduction*,
§ 4.

                                                              6—2

Israel began Azariah son of Amaziah king of Judah to
2 reign. Sixteen years old was he when he began to reign;
and he reigned two and fifty years in Jerusalem: and his
3 mother's name was Jecoliah of Jerusalem. And he did
that which was right in the eyes of the LORD, according
4 to all that his father Amaziah had done. Howbeit the
high places were not taken away: the people still sacrificed and burnt incense in the high places.

xv. 5. *Azariah's leprosy.*

5 And the LORD smote the king, so that he was a leper
unto the day of his death, and dwelt in a several house.
And Jotham the king's son was over the household,
judging the people of the land.

xv. 6, 7. *Conclusion.*

6 Now the rest of the acts of Azariah, and all that he did,

Azariah appears to be the form of the name peculiar to
Kings (in *vv.* 13, 30, 32, 34 of this chapter the true reading, as
shown by the LXX, is *Azariah*). Elsewhere (Isaiah, Amos,
Hosea, Chronicles) the form is *Uzziah*, with the exception of
the list of Judaean kings in 1 Chron. iii. 14 (where *Azariah* is
given).

5. This *v.* is probably an abridgement based upon the Judaean
annalistic document.

in a several house: i.e. in a house by himself, isolated;
margin 'in a lazar house.' This rendering, however, is highly
doubtful. By a different division of the Hebrew letters the
meaning can be obtained: 'in his own house at liberty.' This
is probably right. Though certainly isolated, and only govern-
ing through a regent, the king was allowed to live in his own
house unmolested, whereas ordinary lepers were expelled from
the city.

Jotham etc. How long Jotham's regency lasted is uncertain.
One of the ways in which the chronological difficulties can be
reduced is to assume that the greater part of the sixteen years'
reign assigned to Jotham (*v.* 33) were spent in this regency.
See *Introduction*, § 4.

judging: i.e. exercising royal functions.

6, 7. the rest of the acts etc.: the Chronicler mentions his
wars with the Philistines and Arabs, his reorganization of the

are they not written in the book of the chronicles of the
kings of Judah? And Azariah slept with his fathers; and 7
they buried him with his fathers in the city of David:
and Jotham his son reigned in his stead.

XV. 8–12. ZECHARIAH OF ISRAEL.

xv. 8, 9. *Introduction.*

In the thirty and eighth year of Azariah king of Judah 8
did Zechariah the son of Jeroboam reign over Israel in
Samaria six months.   And he did that which was evil 9
in the sight of the LORD, as his fathers had done: he
departed not from the sins of Jeroboam the son of
Nebat, wherewith he made Israel to sin.

xv. 10. *The conspiracy of Shallum.*

And Shallum the son of Jabesh conspired against him, 10
and smote him before the people, and slew him, and
reigned in his stead.

xv. 11, 12. *Conclusion.*

Now the rest of the acts of Zechariah, behold, they are 11
written in the book of the chronicles of the kings of
Israel.   This was the word of the LORD which he spake 12

---

army and the defences of the capital, and his promotion of
agriculture etc.

8–12.   The death of the great king Jeroboam II was followed
by a period of anarchy in north Israel.   A succession of usurpers
brought the country to its final doom, ending in the destruction
of Samaria (722 B.C.).   A vivid picture of the disorders of the
time is given in the prophecies of Hosea.

8.   the thirty and eighth year: this *datum* can only be
reconciled with xiv. 23 either by altering the number here to
'in the twenty-seventh year,' or by lengthening the reign of
Jeroboam to fifty-two years.

10.   This verse is probably based upon the annalistic document.

before the people: read with LXX (Luc.) 'in Ibleam.'   For
Ibleam, see ix. 27 and note.

12.   This was the word of the Lord etc.: cf. x. 30.   The
proper position of this verse, which may have been added by
a later editor, is immediately after *v.* 10.

unto Jehu, saying, Thy sons to the fourth generation
shall sit upon the throne of Israel. And so it came to
pass.

XV. 13–16. SHALLUM OF ISRAEL.

xv. 13. *Introduction.*

13 Shallum the son of Jabesh began to reign in the nine
and thirtieth year of Uzziah king of Judah; and he
reigned the space of a month in Samaria.

xv. 14. *Menahem seizes the throne.*

14 And Menahem the son of Gadi went up from Tirzah,
and came to Samaria, and smote Shallum the son of
Jabesh in Samaria, and slew him, and reigned in his
stead.

xv. 15. *Conclusion.*

15 Now the rest of the acts of Shallum, and his conspiracy
which he made, behold, they are written in the book of
the chronicles of the kings of Israel.

xv. 16. *Appended notice regarding Menahem.*

16 Then Menahem smote Tiphsah, and all that were
therein, and the borders thereof, from Tirzah: because

13–16. Shallum reigned but one month. Possibly, as Kittel
has suggested, the possession of the throne was contested by
two rival parties, one under Shallum in Samaria, the other
under Menahem, who held Tirzah the ancient capital.

14. This verse is based probably upon the annalistic document, from which also *v.* 16 was doubtless derived.

Tirzah was for some time the capital of the northern kingdom
(cf. 1 Kings xv. 21, xvi. 15 etc.), and probably lay a few miles
from Shechem; but its exact site has not been fixed.

16. The verse is clearly out of place. Its natural position
would be immediately after *v.* 14.

Tiphsah: no Palestinian town of this name is known. It
obviously cannot be the *Tiphsah* which lay on the Euphrates
(1 Kings iv. 24). The LXX (Luc.) reads the name differently;
probably the text is an error for *Tappuah*, a town on the borders
of Ephraim and Manasseh (Josh. xvi. 8, cf. xvii. 7). The reason
for Menahem's attack was doubtless that the place was held by
the partisans of Shallum, and refused to recognize Menahem,
who marched against it from Tirzah.

they opened not to him, therefore he smote it; and all
the women therein that were with child he ripped up.

XV. 17–22. MENAHEM OF ISRAEL.

xv. 17, 18. *Introduction.*

In the nine and thirtieth year of Azariah king of Judah 17
began Menahem the son of Gadi to reign over Israel,
and reigned ten years in Samaria. And he did that 18
which was evil in the sight of the LORD: he departed
not all his days from the sins of Jeroboam the son of
Nebat, wherewith he made Israel to sin.

xv. 19, 20. *Tiglath-Pileser invades Israel.*

There came against the land Pul the king of Assyria; 19
and Menahem gave Pul a thousand talents of silver, that

17–22. Menahem is mentioned in an Assyrian inscription by
Tiglath-Pileser as paying tribute, with other kings, to him in
the eighth year of his reign (= 738 B.C.). The Hebrew version
of this incident is given in *vv.* 19 f., from which it appears that
Tiglath-Pileser had actually invaded the territories of Israel.
Menahem was accepted as a tributary-prince, and 'confirmed'
in the possession of the throne, apparently against a rival party
in Israel, by the Assyrian monarch, who withdrew his forces.
This must have taken place in the latter part of Menahem's
reign, according to the chronology necessitated by the Assyrian
dates.

18. **all his days**: this phrase occurs in the Hebrew text at
the end of the verse, and (with a slight alteration) is attached
by the LXX to the opening of *v.* 19. Read with LXX 'In his
days came against the land' etc.

19, 20. These verses are derived from the annalistic document.

19. **Pul**: though both names are used in this chapter (cf.
v. 29) the evidence of the Assyrian inscriptions makes it certain
that Pul and Tiglath-Pileser are identical (in 1 Chron. v. 26
they are distinguished). It has been conjectured that *Pul*
(Assyr. *Pulu*) is the real name of the king, who was a usurper,
and that he assumed the name of *Tiglath-Pileser* when he seized
the throne.

a thousand talents of silver: about £375,000 or more.

his hand might be with him to confirm the kingdom in
20 his hand. And Menahem exacted the money of Israel,
even of all the mighty men of wealth, of each man fifty
shekels of silver, to give to the king of Assyria. So the
king of Assyria turned back, and stayed not there in the
land.

xv. 21, 22. Conclusion.

21 Now the rest of the acts of Menahem, and all that he
did, are they not written in the book of the chronicles
22 of the kings of Israel? And Menahem slept with his
fathers ; and Pekahiah his son reigned in his stead.

XV. 23–26. PEKAHIAH OF ISRAEL.
xv. 23, 24. Introduction.

23   In the fiftieth year of Azariah king of Judah Pekahiah
the son of Menahem began to reign over Israel in
24 Samaria, *and reigned* two years. And he did that which
was evil in the sight of the LORD : he departed not from
the sins of Jeroboam the son of Nebat, wherewith he
made Israel to sin.

xv. 25. Conspiracy of Pekah.

25 And Pekah the son of Remaliah, his captain, conspired
against him, and smote him in Samaria, in the castle of

---

20. exacted etc.: or rather 'imposed (lit. brought forth) the
money upon Israel': but the phraseology is strange. Perhaps
the text should be emended so as to read, 'and Menahem commanded all Israel, even all the mighty men of wealth, to give
to the king of Assyria, each man fifty shekels.'

mighty men of wealth : i.e. well-to-do people. If the talent
is reckoned at 3000 shekels, this would mean that some 60,000
contributed fifty shekels each.

23. two years : this is certainly correct, as the Assyrian dates
show : LXX (Luc.) has 'ten years,' which is assumed as the
length of this reign in xvii. 1.

25.   This verse is based on the annalistic document.

his captain : or rather adjutant ; cf. vii. 2 and note.

in the castle of the king's house : i.e. in the citadel (keep)

the king's house, with Argob and Arieh ; and with him
were fifty men of the Gileadites : and he slew him, and
reigned in his stead.

xv. 26. *Conclusion.*

Now the rest of the acts of Pekahiah, and all that he did, 26
behold, they are written in the book of the chronicles of
the kings of Israel.

XV. 27-31. PEKAH OF ISRAEL.

xv. 27, 28. *Introduction.*

In the two and fiftieth year of Azariah king of Judah 27

---

of the royal palace : some central strongly fortified part of the
royal buildings is probably meant ; cf. 1 Kings xvi. 18.

with Argob and Arieh : 'Argob' is the name of a district in
Bashan (1 Kings iv. 13) ; the other word means 'the lion.' The
text is hopelessly corrupt. Perhaps the best suggestion that has
been made is that the clause has been inserted by mistake in
its present position and really belongs to *v.* 29 ; then the names
would denote certain districts which were depopulated by Tiglath-Pileser (read ? 'Argob and Havvoth-jair' ; cf. Deut. iii. 14).

of the Gileadites : Pekah may, therefore, have been himself
a Gileadite.

27-31. The party which raised Pekah to the throne was
doubtless the anti-Assyrian faction. Pekahiah, like his father,
had ruled as vassal of the Assyrian king, supported by the
party in Israel which was favourable to Assyria. This party
again was represented by Hoshea, who murdered Pekah, and
was loyal to Assyria. This state of affairs will explain the
proceedings of Pekah and his allies, and also the consequent
punitive expedition of Tiglath-Pileser, described in *v.* 29. It
appears that an anti-Assyrian coalition of Syrian states was
organized by Pekah of Israel and Rezin of Damascus. The
unwillingness of Judah, under Ahaz, to join this confederacy
was the immediate cause of the Syro-Ephraimitish war described
in *v.* 37 and xvi. 5 f. This was followed by Tiglath-Pileser's
expedition (in 734 or 733 B.C.). Damascus was captured, and
north Israel punished (as described in *v.* 29), Pekah being
deposed and slain, and Hoshea, the nominee of Tiglath-Pileser,
being raised to the throne in his stead. The Assyrian dates,
it should be noted, make a twenty years' reign for Pekah (*v.* 27)
impossible.

27. two and fiftieth : this should rather be 'fifty-first,' since
the second year of Pekah = the first of Jotham according to
v. 32.

Pekah the son of Remaliah began to reign over Israel
28 in Samaria, *and reigned* twenty years. And he did that
which was evil in the sight of the LORD: he departed
not from the sins of Jeroboam the son of Nebat, wherewith he made Israel to sin.

xv. 29, 30. *The northern districts of Israel seized by
Tiglath-Pileser; murder of Pekah.*

29 In the days of Pekah king of Israel came Tiglath-pileser
king of Assyria, and took Ijon, and Abel-beth-maacah,
and Janoah, and Kedesh, and Hazor, and Gilead, and
Galilee, all the land of Naphtali; and he carried them
30 captive to Assyria. And Hoshea the son of Elah made
a conspiracy against Pekah the son of Remaliah, and

---

twenty years: the Assyrian dates make it necessary to find
room for part of the reign of Menahem, and the whole of those
of Pekahiah and Pekah between 738 and 732 B.C. (see *Introduction*, § 4). The reign of Pekah can at most have lasted only
four years.

29. The towns and districts mentioned lay in the extreme
north; cf. 1 Kings xv. 20, from which it appears that the same
district was ravaged by the Syrians in the time of Asa. **Ijon**
may be the modern *Tell Dibbîn*, a little hill rising on 'the plain
of '*Ayûn*' (*Merj 'Ayûn*) between the valleys of the Litani and
upper Jordan; a little to the south lies '*Abil*, which probably
marks the position of the district of **Abel-beth-maacah**; the site
of **Janoah** cannot be fixed, but it must have been in the same
district; **Kedesh** is the modern *Ḳades* north-west of Lake Huleh;
Hazor lay not far from Kedesh in the extreme north of the territory of Naphtali; **Galilee** ('the Circuit') appears to have been
more or less co-extensive with the territory of Naphtali; it was
only later that the name was extended to the entire district north
of the plain of Esdraelon; **Gilead**—unless the form of the name
is corrupt—must be the name of another town in this northern
district; it cannot here denote the trans-Jordanic district.

carried them captive: or rather 'exiled them,' i.e. deported
the Israelitish population.

30. Hoshea: the leader of the party favourable to Assyria.
Tiglath-Pileser allowed him to reign, after receiving tribute from
him (according to the royal annals preserved in the Assyrian
inscription).

smote him, and slew him, and reigned in his stead, in the twentieth year of Jotham the son of Uzziah.

xv. 31. *Conclusion.*

Now the rest of the acts of Pekah, and all that he did, 31 behold, they are written in the book of the chronicles of the kings of Israel.

XV. 32-38. JOTHAM OF JUDAH (cf. 2 Chron. xxvii.).

xv. 32-35. *Introduction.*

In the second year of Pekah the son of Remaliah king 32 of Israel began Jotham the son of Uzziah king of Judah to reign.   Five and twenty years old was he when he 33 began to reign; and he reigned sixteen years in Jerusalem: and his mother's name was Jerusha the daughter of Zadok.   And he did that which was right in the eyes 34 of the LORD: he did according to all that his father Uzziah had done.   Howbeit the high places were not 35 taken away: the people still sacrificed and burned incense in the high places.   He built the upper gate of the house of the LORD.

---

in the twentieth year of Jotham etc. : the date is inconsistent with xvii. 1, and, moreover, only sixteen years are assigned to Jotham's reign (xvi. 1).   The clause is probably an incorrect (or corrupt) gloss.   The annalistic document never dates events by the reigns of the sister kingdom.

32-38.   The section includes notices of Jotham's building 'the upper gate' of the Temple (*v.* 35 *b*), and of the outbreak of the Syro-Ephraimitish war (*v.* 37).   Both are based on the annalistic document; the rest of the section is from the compiler's hand.   From the account of Jotham's reign in Chronicles it would appear that he continued the successful administration of his father Uzziah.

35.   the upper gate etc.: little is known of the gates of Solomon's Temple.   Jeremiah mentions an 'upper gate of Benjamin' (Jer. xx. 2), and a 'new gate' (xxvi. 10; the 'third entry' of xxxviii. 14 is probably a textual error for 'gate of the body-guard' which may be identical with the 'new gate').   Of these the gate of Benjamin lay on the north of the Temple-court, and may be identical with 'the upper gate' here (cf. the 'northern

xv. 36-38. *Conclusion.*

36 Now the rest of the acts of Jotham, and all that he did,
are they not written in the book of the chronicles of the
37 kings of Judah? In those days the LORD began to send
against Judah Rezin the king of Syria, and Pekah the
38 son of Remaliah. And Jotham slept with his fathers,
and was buried with his fathers in the city of David his
father: and Ahaz his son reigned in his stead.

XVI. AHAZ OF JUDAH (cf. 2 Chron. xxviii.).

xvi. 1-4. *Introduction.*

16   In the seventeenth year of Pekah the son of Remaliah
Ahaz the son of Jotham king of Judah began to reign.
2 Twenty years old was Ahaz when he began to reign;
and he reigned sixteen years in Jerusalem: and he did
not that which was right in the eyes of the LORD his
3 God, like David his father. But he walked in the way
of the kings of Israel, yea, and made his son to pass

---

gate' of Ezek. viii. 3). The 'new gate' may have been the
southern one (in the south wall of the Temple-court) communi-
cating directly between the palace and the Temple (= 'the gate
of the guard,' xi. 19).

37. In those days etc.: cf. xvi. 5 f. and notes.

xvi. 2. Twenty years old etc.: if Ahaz reigned sixteen years
he must have died at the age of thirty-five or thirty-six; according
to xviii. 2, Hezekiah, at his accession, was twenty-five years old,
and consequently must have been born when his father (Ahaz)
was ten years old! Some of the numbers must obviously be
wrong. (See *Introduction,* § 4.)

3. made his son to pass etc.: the expression undoubtedly
refers to child-sacrifice by actual burning, the offering being made
to Jehovah, not to any foreign god. This appalling rite seems to
have been an old Semitic one; it was not unknown in ancient
Israel (cf. Judges xi. 34 f.), and survived among the immediate
neighbours of the Hebrews (cf. iii. 27). In the latter period of
the Judaean monarchy it was revived in Judah (cf. xxi. 6, xxiii.
10; Micah vi. 7; Jer. vii. 31, xix. 5 etc.), apparently when the
nation was conscious of pressing dangers and anxieties. It was
one of the signs of the decline and fall of the state and the
national religion. Ahaz seems to be blamed in this passage for
the re-introduction of this evil feature into the state religion.

through the fire, according to the abominations of the heathen, whom the LORD cast out from before the children of Israel.   And he sacrificed and burnt incense in 4 the high places, and on the hills, and under every green tree.

xvi. 5-9.   *The Syro-Ephraimite attack on Judah.*

Then Rezin king of Syria and Pekah son of Remaliah 5 king of Israel came up to Jerusalem to war: and they besieged Ahaz, but could not overcome him.   At that 6 time Rezin king of Syria recovered Elath to Syria, and drave the Jews from Elath: and the Syrians came to Elath, and dwelt there, unto this day.   So Ahaz sent 7 messengers to Tiglath-pileser king of Assyria, saying, I am thy servant and thy son: come up, and save me out of the hand of the king of Syria, and out of the

4.   And he sacrificed…incense: i.e. not merely tolerated such practices as his predecessors had done, but personally participated in them.

hills…green tree: the phraseology recalls that of Jeremiah; cf. Jer. ii. 30, iii. 6.

5-9.   Apparently the war had already broken out in Jotham's reign (cf. xv. 37); but the crisis only became acute after Ahaz had ascended the throne.   Possibly, however, the attack on Jerusalem took the Judaeans by surprise—it certainly produced the greatest consternation there (cf. Is. vii. 1 f.).   In any case it failed in its object, the only result being that Ahaz, against the emphatic advice of Isaiah, appealed for protection to Tiglath-Pileser.   The section is probably based upon the annalistic document.

5.   This verse agrees verbally with Is. vii. 1.   Rezin is mentioned in the Assyrian record as one of the princes who paid tribute with Menahem to Tiglath-Pileser in 738.

6.   the Syrians etc.: the Masoretes (the Rabbinic editors of the Heb. text) read 'the Edomites' (the two names are very similar in Hebrew); accepting this as undoubtedly right, we must correct 'Syria' in the rest of the verse to 'Edom,' and delete 'Rezin.'   What is stated is that the Edomites (taking advantage of Judah's difficulties) recovered the port of Elath, which they had previously lost (cf. xiv. 22).   This agrees with 2 Chron. xxviii. 17.   Syria had never been in possession of Elath.

7, 8.   Ahaz sends a submissive message together with tribute ('a present') to Tiglath-Pileser.

hand of the king of Israel, which rise up against me.
8 And Ahaz took the silver and gold that was found in the
house of the LORD, and in the treasures of the king's
house, and sent it for a present to the king of Assyria.
9 And the king of Assyria hearkened unto him: and the
king of Assyria went up against Damascus, and took
it, and carried *the people of* it captive to Kir, and slew
Rezin.

xvi. 10–16. *Ahaz orders the erection of a new altar in the Temple.*

10 And king Ahaz went to Damascus to meet Tiglath-pileser
king of Assyria, and saw the altar that was at Damascus:
and king Ahaz sent to Urijah the priest the fashion of
the altar, and the pattern of it, according to all the work-
11 manship thereof.   And Urijah the priest built an altar:
according to all that king Ahaz had sent from Damascus,
so did Urijah the priest make it against king Ahaz came
12 from Damascus.   And when the king was come from

------

9.   against Damascus etc.: the inscriptions of Tiglath-Pileser
record that two successive expeditions in the years 733 and
732 B.C. were necessary before Damascus was subdued, but do
not record the actual capture of the city or the death of Rezin.
The expedition against north Israel described in xv. 29 preceded
this.

to Kir: cf. Amos i. 5: LXX omits here (perhaps rightly).   It
is mentioned in connexion with Elam in Is. xxii. 6, but its exact
position is unknown.

10–16.   After the capture of Damascus, Tiglath-Pileser seems
to have held a court there, which the vassal-princes were required
to attend.   This will explain Ahaz's visit to the city, where he
was apparently detained for some time.   The section, which was
probably derived from the 'Temple-history' (cf. note on xii. 4–
16), gives the impression that Ahaz took an artistic interest in
ritual, and was well versed in its details and requirements.   It
also illustrates how completely the Temple was still a part of the
royal establishment, under the personal control of the king.
Notice especially that the king himself directs alterations to be
made in the ritual, and consecrates the new altar.

10.   the altar: viz. that of the principal Temple.

Urijah the priest is mentioned in Is. viii. 2.

Damascus, the king saw the altar: and the king drew
near unto the altar, and offered thereon.   And he burnt 13
his burnt offering and his meal offering, and poured his
drink offering, and sprinkled the blood of his peace
offerings, upon the altar.   And the brasen altar, which 14
was before the LORD, he brought from the forefront of
the house, from between his altar and the house of the
LORD, and put it on the north side of his altar.   And 15
king Ahaz commanded Urijah the priest, saying, Upon
the great altar burn the morning burnt offering, and the
evening meal offering, and the king's burnt offering, and
his meal offering, with the burnt offering of all the people
of the land, and their meal offering, and their drink
offerings; and sprinkle upon it all the blood of the burnt
offering, and all the blood of the sacrifice: but the brasen
altar shall be for me to inquire by.   Thus did Urijah the 16
priest, according to all that king Ahaz commanded.

---

12. and offered thereon: or rather 'went up upon it' (margin),
i.e. ascended to it (possibly by a slope leading to a ledge; the
altar would be too high for the officiant to celebrate at it, unless
he was raised in some way; steps were forbidden, cf. Ex. xx. 26).
Cf. xxiii. 9.

13.   At a solemn function, like that described, the king would
officiate in person; but ordinarily the sacrifices (including the
king's) would be offered by the priest (cf. *v.* 15).   In the
same way Uzziah also exercised priestly functions (cf. 2 Chron.
xxvi. 16).

14.   The verse describes how the new altar supplanted the
old, which was removed so as to be 'between his [the new] altar
and the house of the Lord [i.e. the Temple].'

15. Upon the great altar: i.e. the new altar.   This was to
replace the old for all ordinary sacrifices, while the old (bronze)
altar was reserved for the king **to inquire by**.   What this
expression exactly means is uncertain.   Possibly examination of
portions of the sacrifice, a common Babylonian form of divination
(cf. Ezek. xxi. 21), is intended.   Ahaz may have introduced this
foreign custom into the state-religion.   It should be noted that
the morning burnt offering and **the evening meal offering** are
spoken of.   Apparently there was no 'evening burnt offering' at
this time (cf. Ezek. xlvi. 13–15).

xvi. 17, 18. *The Temple despoiled.*

17 And king Ahaz cut off the borders of the bases, and
removed the laver from off them; and took down the
sea from off the brasen oxen that were under it, and put
18 it upon a pavement of stone.   And the covered way for
the sabbath that they had built in the house, and the
king's entry without, turned he unto the house of the
LORD, because of the king of Assyria.

xvi. 19, 20. *Conclusion.*

19 Now the rest of the acts of Ahaz which he did, are they
not written in the book of the chronicles of the kings of
20 Judah?   And Ahaz slept with his fathers, and was buried
with his fathers in the city of David: and Hezekiah his
son reigned in his stead.

17, 18.   The annual tribute exacted by Tiglath-Pileser forced
Ahaz to avail himself of the valuable material to be found in the
ornaments and furniture of the Temple.   These verses may also
come from the ' Temple-history.'
    17.   the borders of the bases : or, perhaps, ' the panels of the
stands ': the ' bases ' or ' stands ' here referred to were carriages
(on wheels) which supported lavers; the ' borders' were, perhaps,
the upper and lower metal bars of the frame of the carriage, or
possibly metal 'panels,' which could be detached without ruining
the structure.   Cf. 1 Kings vii. 27 f.   The metal was required for
money purposes.
    the sea from off the brasen oxen : i.e. the huge circular basin
supported on twelve bronze oxen; cf. 1 Kings vii. 23 f.
    18.   the covered way for the sabbath : LXX has 'and the
foundation of the chair (=? throne) he built in the house of the
Lord.'   The details of the verse are obscure.   The final words,
because of the king of Assyria, would be more appropriate at
the end of *v.* 17.
    xvii. 1–6.   The middle part of this section presents a difficult
historical problem.   It appears to assert that Hoshea, who had
come to the throne as the nominee of Tiglath-Pileser (xv. 30),
revolted against Shalmaneser IV and was reduced (xvii. 3),
again revolted and was deposed and made prisoner (xvii. 4) ;
and that this was followed by the siege and fall of Samaria.
But it is difficult to suppose that Hoshea revolted twice, and
that Shalmaneser undertook two (or three) campaigns against

XVII. 1-6. HOSHEA OF ISRAEL.

xvii. 1, 2. *Introduction.*

In the twelfth year of Ahaz king of Judah began **17**
Hoshea the son of Elah to reign in Samaria over Israel,
and reigned nine years. And he did that which was evil **2**
in the sight of the LORD, yet not as the kings of Israel
that were before him.

xvii. 3-6. *The fall of Israel.*

Against him came up Shalmaneser king of Assyria; and **3**
Hoshea became his servant, and brought him presents.
And the king of Assyria found conspiracy in Hoshea; **4**
for he had sent messengers to So king of Egypt, and
offered no present to the king of Assyria, as he had done

Israel during his short reign (727–722)—the Assyrian records
only mention one—and finally that Hoshea had been imprisoned
by the Assyrian king before the siege began. The best solution
of the difficulty seems to be to suppose that two parallel but independent narratives of the same events have been combined, one
of which (*vv.* 3, 4) describes the fate of the king, and the second
(*vv.* 5, 6 = xviii. 9–11) the fate of the capital.

1. the twelfth year of Ahaz: the chronology implies a ten-
years' reign of Pekahiah; cf. xv. 23 and note.

2. yet not as the kings etc.: the grounds for this favourable
reservation are not given.

3. became his servant: i.e. submitted to him. The expedition of Shalmaneser falls in the years 724–722. Apparently
Hoshea hastened to meet the Assyrian king, and tendered his
submission in the usual manner, i.e. by paying tribute; and this
was accepted.

4. conspiracy: LXX 'treachery.' After tendering his submission Hoshea engaged in treasonable negotiations. It is
possible, however, to construe *vv.* 3 *b* and 4 *a* as a retrospect-
ive parenthesis: 'Against him came up Shalmaneser king of
Assyria (now Hoshea had been his servant [vassal], and
brought him tribute; but the king of Assyria had found
conspiracy etc.).'

So king of Egypt is usually identified with Sabako the
Ethiopian monarch who founded the twenty-fifth dynasty in
Egypt; but more probably the name should be read *Sevê king
of Musri*, i.e. the general of the north-Arabian kingdom of
Musri.

year by year: therefore the king of Assyria shut him
5 up, and bound him in prison. Then the king of Assyria
came up throughout all the land, and went up to Samaria,
6 and besieged it three years. In the ninth year of Hoshea,
the king of Assyria took Samaria, and carried Israel
away unto Assyria, and placed them in Halah, and in
Habor, *on* the river of Gozan, and in the cities of the
Medes.

---

shut him up: lit. 'hindered him,' i.e. detained him in
custody, having found him guilty of disloyalty. Thus according
to this account Hoshea was under arrest before the siege of
Samaria was begun.

6. In the ninth year etc.: since Hoshea came to the throne
in 732 B.C. his ninth year would be 724 B.C., two years before
Samaria fell (722 B.C.). The statement is thus a miscalculation
of the compiler. Shalmaneser, however, died before the capture
of the city, which was actually taken by Sargon.

carried Israel away etc.: according to Sargon's own statement 27,290 of the inhabitants were deported.

Halah: if a district is meant it may perhaps be identical with
the Mesopotamian Chalkitis, which is mentioned by Ptolemaeus
with Gauzanitis. The LXX, however, takes it to be the name
of a river, in which case it may, perhaps, be a mistake for *Baliḥ*,
a tributary of the Euphrates west of the Habur.

Habor is the modern *Ḥabūr* (the Chaboras of the Greeks), a
northern tributary of the Euphrates.

Gozan is the Assyrian *Guzannu* (= Gauzanitis), a province of
Mesopotamia adjoining the upper waters of the *Ḥabūr*.

7–23. The end of the northern kingdom affords an opportunity
for some characteristic comments and reflections by the compiler.
The ruin of the State is regarded as the fitting climax of, and
appropriate punishment for, a course of unbroken apostasy from
Jehovah. The indictment enumerates the adoption of the worship
at the high places and its concomitant idolatry, the introduction
of foreign cults (star-worship, the cultus of the Phoenician Baal,
child-sacrifice); and the evil influence of 'Jeroboam the son of
Nebat' in establishing the worship of the golden calves is once
again emphasized.

It is clear from *vv.* 19, 20 that the section in its present form
cannot be earlier than the Exile, since the downfall of Judah is
pre-supposed. The epilogue, as a whole, seems to be the work
of the later Deuteronomic compiler, who wrote during the Exile.
He has, however, incorporated a fragment of a section written by
the earlier compiler (*vv.* 18 and 21–23).

XVII. 7–23. REFLECTIONS ON THE HISTORY AND FATE
OF THE NORTHERN KINGDOM.

And it was so, because the children of Israel had sinned 7
against the LORD their God, which brought them up out
of the land of Egypt from under the hand of Pharaoh
king of Egypt, and had feared other gods, and walked 8
in the statutes of the nations, whom the LORD cast out
from before the children of Israel, and of the kings of
Israel, which they made.   And the children of Israel did 9
secretly things that were not right against the LORD
their God, and they built them high places in all their
cities, from the tower of the watchmen to the fenced city.
And they set them up pillars and Asherim upon every 10
high hill, and under every green tree: and there they 11
burnt incense in all the high places, as did the nations
whom the LORD carried away before them; and wrought
wicked things to provoke the LORD to anger: and they 12
served idols, whereof the LORD had said unto them, Ye
shall not do this thing.   Yet the LORD testified unto 13
Israel, and unto Judah, by the hand of every prophet,
and of every seer, saying, Turn ye from your evil ways,
and keep my commandments and my statutes, according
to all the law which I commanded your fathers, and

---

7. **And it was so, because**: read with LXX (Luc.) 'and the
wrath of Jehovah was on Israel because.'

9. **did secretly**: read, perhaps, 'and devised.'

from the tower of the watchmen etc. : i.e. wherever men were,
from the solitary tower to the embattled city; cf. xviii. 8.

10. **pillars and Asherim**: cf. 1 Kings xiv. 23. The 'pillars'
(Heb. *maṣṣēbôth*) were a survival from old Semitic worship.
Originally regarded as the abode of the deity, they were, later,
retained as symbols of the same.   On the 'Asherim' (pl. of
Asherah) or sacred poles, cf. xiii. 6 and note.

high hill etc.: cf. xiv. 4 and note.

11. **burnt incense**: cf. xiv. 4 and note.

13. **Yet the Lord testified** etc.: cf. Jer. vii. 25, xi. 7, xviii.
11, xxv. 4 f., xxxv. 15, xxxvi. 3, 7 : 'and of every seer' is
probably a gloss.

which I sent to you by the hand of my servants the
14 prophets.   Notwithstanding they would not hear, but
hardened their neck, like to the neck of their fathers,
15 who believed not in the LORD their God.   And they
rejected his statutes, and his covenant that he made with
their fathers, and his testimonies which he testified unto
them ; and they followed vanity, and became vain, and
went after the nations that were round about them,
concerning whom the LORD had charged them that they
16 should not do like them.   And they forsook all the
commandments of the LORD their God, and made them
molten images, even two calves, and made an Asherah,
and worshipped all the host of heaven, and served Baal.
17 And they caused their sons and their daughters to pass
through the fire, and used divination and enchantments,
and sold themselves to do that which was evil in the
18 sight of the LORD, to provoke him to anger.   Therefore
the LORD was very angry with Israel, and removed them
out of his sight : there was none left but the tribe of
19 Judah only.   Also Judah kept not the commandments
of the LORD their God, but walked in the statutes of
20 Israel which they made.   And the LORD rejected all the

---

14.   would not hear : cf. Jer. vii. 26 etc.

hardened their neck : cf. Jer. vii. 26, xvii. 23 (Deut. x. 16).

15.   followed vanity...vain : cf. Jer. ii. 5.

16.   even two calves : probably an incorrect gloss on ' molten images,' which expression includes image worship generally.

all the host of heaven : i.e. astral worship ; cf. xxi. 3 and note.

17.   caused their sons etc. : cf. xvi. 3 and note.

18.   the tribe of Judah only : cf. 1 Kings xii. 20.   This correctly represents the old tradition ; the tribe of Benjamin, as a whole, seems to have gone with the northern kingdom.

19, 20.   These verses interrupt the connexion between *vv.* 18 and 21-23, which probably are the work of the original Deuteronomic compiler.   On this view *vv.* 19, 20, which qualify *v.* 18, may be assigned to the writer of *vv.* 7-17, i.e. to the second compiler.

seed of Israel, and afflicted them, and delivered them
into the hand of spoilers, until he had cast them out of
his sight.   For he rent Israel from the house of David; 21
and they made Jeroboam the son of Nebat king: and
Jeroboam drave Israel from following the LORD, and
made them sin a great sin.   And the children of Israel 22
walked in all the sins of Jeroboam which he did; they
departed not from them; until the LORD removed Israel 23
out of his sight, as he spake by the hand of all his
servants the prophets.   So Israel was carried away out
of their own land to Assyria, unto this day.

XVII. 24–34 *a*, 41.   THE RE-PEOPLING OF THE LAND.

(*a*) xvii. 24–28.   *Foreign settlers introduced into Samaria*

And the king of Assyria brought men from Babylon, 24
and from Cuthah, and from Avva, and from Hamath and

21–23.   These verses trace the fall of the northern kingdom to
one simple cause, the sin of 'Jeroboam the son of Nebat,' in
accordance with the reiterated statement of the author of the
framework, i.e. the original Deuteronomic compiler.

24–41.   The section describes (*a*) the repeopling of the conquered
province by colonists from distant parts of the empire (*vv.* 24–
28); (*b*) the cultus of the new settlers (*vv.* 29–34 *a*, 41); these
are followed (*c*) by a passage (*vv.* 34 *b*–40) which has no obvious
connexion with what precedes, denouncing the sins of the northern
kingdom generally.   Not improbably all three passages are derived
from different sources; (*a*) may be based on the annals of north
Israel, (*b*) may, perhaps, be assigned to the younger (exilic)
compiler, and (*c*) to a later writer.

24–28.   This passage describes how foreign colonists were settled
in Samaria by Sargon.   It has been maintained, however, that the
incident described really occurred in the reign of Asshur-bani-pal
(668–626 B.C.), some seventy years after the time of Sargon (viz.
in 648 B.C.).   It is true that according to Ezra iv. 10 and 2 the
Samaritans traced their origin to 'the great and noble Osnappar'
(i.e. Asshur-bani-pal), and also to Esar-haddon.   But this fact
does not exclude an earlier colonization by Sargon.   Apparently
there were successive colonizations.

24.   the king of Assyria : this might mean Asshur-bani-pal,
but probably refers to Sargon.

Cuthah (in *v.* 30 'Cuth')=the *Kutū* of the Assyrian inscriptions, and is identified with the ruined site now known as *Tell*

Sepharvaim, and placed them in the cities of Samaria
instead of the children of Israel: and they possessed
25 Samaria, and dwelt in the cities thereof. And so it was,
at the beginning of their dwelling there, that they feared
not the LORD: therefore the LORD sent lions among
26 them, which killed some of them. Wherefore they
spake to the king of Assyria, saying, The nations which
thou hast carried away, and placed in the cities of Samaria, know not the manner of the God of the land:
therefore he hath sent lions among them, and, behold,
they slay them, because they know not the manner of
27 the God of the land. Then the king of Assyria commanded, saying, Carry thither one of the priests whom
ye brought from thence; and let them go and dwell
there, and let him teach them the manner of the God of
28 the land. So one of the priests whom they had carried
away from Samaria came and dwelt in Beth-el, and
taught them how they should fear the LORD.

Ibrāhim, north-east of Babylon. By Josephus and the later Jews
the Samaritans were called 'Cuthaeans.'

Avva, in xviii. 34 called 'Ivvah,' has not been identified. It
was no doubt a town in Syria.

Hamath: i.e. the city of that name on the Orontes; cf. xiv. 25
and note.

Sepharvaim, both here and in xviii. 34, appears to be the
name of a Syrian town, perhaps *Shabarain* (=? *Sibraim* of
Ezek. xlvii. 16), which was conquered by Shalmaneser IV (727–
722 B.C.). It has been suggested, however, that Sepharvaim
is really the Babylonian city *Sippara* (between the Euphrates
and Tigris). Thus, according to the present passage, colonists
from Babylonia and Syria were brought by Sargon to Samaria.
Winckler, however, supposes that in the original form of this
passage only colonists from Babylonia were spoken of (Babylon,
Cuthah and Sippara); he thinks Hamath and Avva have been
added by mistake (from xix. 13).

26. the manner etc.: i.e. the appointed worship or cultus.
Each land was supposed to have its own god, who was powerful
in his own domain, and each god had his own special ritual,
without some knowledge of which he could not be approached.

27. whom ye brought: read with LXX (Luc.) 'whom I
exiled': and for 'let them go' etc. read 'let him go' etc.

(*b*) xvii. 29-34 *a*, 41. *Foreign cults of the colonists.*

Howbeit every nation made gods of their own, and put 29
them in the houses of the high places which the Samaritans had made, every nation in their cities wherein
they dwelt. And the men of Babylon made Succoth- 30
benoth, and the men of Cuth made Nergal, and the men
of Hamath made Ashima, and the Avvites made Nibhaz 31
and Tartak, and the Sepharvites burnt their children in
the fire to Adrammelech and Anammelech, the gods of
Sepharvaim. So they feared the LORD, and made unto 32
them from among themselves priests of the high places,
which sacrificed for them in the houses of the high
places. They feared the LORD, and served their own 33
gods, after the manner of the nations from among whom
they had been carried away. Unto this day they do 34
after the former manners:

(*c*) xvii. 34 *b*-40. *The sins of the northern kingdom*
again denounced.

they fear not the LORD, neither do they after their
statutes, or after their ordinances, or after the law or
after the commandment which the LORD commanded

29-34 *a*, **41.** This passage was probably not written till the
Exile by the younger Deuteronomic redactor.

29. in the houses etc.: i.e. in the temples of the different
high places, which constituted the local sanctuaries.

30. Succoth-benoth: no satisfactory explanation of the name
of this deity has yet been given. The natural object of worship
for 'the men of Babylon' would have been their principal god
Marduk (Merodach).

Nergal was the tutelary deity of the city of Cuthah (Kutu); he
was a war-god.

30, 31. The other names of gods here mentioned have not yet
been satisfactorily explained. 'Adrammelech' (cf. xix. 37) and
'Anammelech' are apparently compounds of the well-known
Assyrian divine names Adar and Anu.

34 *a*. **Unto this day**: i.e. probably during the Exile.

34 *b*–**40.** This passage can hardly refer primarily to the mixed
population of Samaria—its opening statement 'they fear not the

35 the children of Jacob, whom he named Israel; with
whom the LORD had made a covenant, and charged them,
saying, Ye shall not fear other gods, nor bow yourselves
36 to them, nor serve them, nor sacrifice to them: but the
LORD, who brought you up out of the land of Egypt with
great power and with a stretched out arm, him shall ye
fear, and unto him shall ye bow yourselves, and to him
37 shall ye sacrifice: and the statutes and the ordinances,
and the law and the commandment, which he wrote for
you, ye shall observe to do for evermore; and ye shall
38 not fear other gods: and the covenant that I have made
with you ye shall not forget; neither shall ye fear other
39 gods: but the LORD your God shall ye fear; and he
shall deliver you out of the hand of all your enemies.
40 Howbeit they did not hearken, but they did after their
41 former manner.   So these nations feared the LORD, and
served their graven images; their children likewise, and
their children's children, as did their fathers, so do they
unto this day.

Lord' directly contradicts *vv.* 32, 33 (and 41)—it seems rather
to be a fresh indictment based upon a survey of the entire history
of the northern kingdom (parallel to *vv.* 7-23), written by a later
(post-exilic) hand.   On the other hand *v.* 41 agrees with the
standpoint of *vv.* 24-28, and may come from the hand of the
earlier compiler.

37. **the law...which he wrote** etc.: i.e. the written Torah.

xviii.-xxv. This long section, which narrates with great
fulness certain critical episodes in the reign of Hezekiah, is
marked by certain striking features.   The larger part of it
recurs in a duplicate text in the Book of Isaiah (xviii. 17-xx. 10
= Is. xxxvi.-xxxix., except that xviii. 12-14 has no equivalent
in Isaiah, and Is. xxxviii. 9-20 ['Hezekiah's Psalm'] is absent
from Kings).   A careful comparison of the duplicate texts shows
that the editor of the Book of Isaiah derived the duplicate chapters
from Kings.   The compiler of Kings probably derived the material
from a biography of Isaiah (similar in character to those of
Elijah and Elisha utilized in the earlier chapters).   In each of
the three episodes contained in this biographical source (Sennacherib's invasion of Judah, Hezekiah's sickness and recovery,

XVIII.–XXV. THE HISTORY OF JUDAH ALONE.

XVIII.–XX. HEZEKIAH AND ISAIAH
(cf. 2 Chron. xxix.–xxxii.).

xviii. 1–8. *Introduction.*

Now it came to pass in the third year of Hoshea son **18**
of Elah king of Israel, that Hezekiah the son of Ahaz
king of Judah began to reign. Twenty and five years **2**
old was he when he began to reign ; and he reigned
twenty and nine years in Jerusalem : and his mother's
name was Abi the daughter of Zechariah. And he did **3**
that which was right in the eyes of the LORD, according
to all that David his father had done. He removed the **4**
high places, and brake the pillars, and cut down the
Asherah : and he brake in pieces the brasen serpent that
Moses had made ; for unto those days the children of

---

the embassy of Merodach-Baladan), Isaiah plays a dominant part.
The source of the narratives may possibly be identical with ' the
vision of Isaiah ' referred to in 2 Chron. xxxii. 32.

xviii. 1–8. These verses, which are mainly the work of the
original compiler, are unusually full. They contain a notice of
the king's measures for the thorough reformation of the national
worship. The 'high places,' i.e. the local sanctuaries, were
suppressed, and the idolatrous symbols, which were still to be
found in the Temple and elsewhere, were destroyed according
to *v.* 4. That a real attempt at reform, in the direction of
purifying the worship of Jehovah, was made by Hezekiah need
not be doubted. It was probably due to the influence of Isaiah,
and may only have taken place after the deliverance of Jerusalem
in 701 B.C., when the prestige and power of the prophet were at
their highest. The centralization of worship in Jerusalem,
however, was only carried out later, at the time of Josiah's
reformation, and very probably *v.* 4*a* is a later addition and
expansion made then after the full reform had been accomplished
(4*b* may be based upon the annalistic document). In any case
Hezekiah's reforming attempt was only temporarily successful.
A violent heathen reaction followed under Manasseh.

1. in the third year : cf. xviii. 9.

2. Abi : or, more correctly, ' Abijah ' (2 Chron. xxix. 1).

4. the Asherah : read the pl. 'the Asherim' with LXX and
Vulg.; cf. xvii. 10, and for Asherah cf. xiii. 6 and note.

the brasen serpent...made : cf. Numb. xxi. 9.

Israel did burn incense to it; and he called it Nehush-
5 tan.   He trusted in the LORD, the God of Israel; so
that after him was none like him among all the kings of
6 Judah, nor *among them* that were before him.   For he
clave to the LORD, he departed not from following him,
but kept his commandments, which the LORD com-
7 manded Moses.   And the LORD was with him; whithderso-
ever he went forth he prospered : and he rebelled against
8 the king of Assyria, and served him not.   He smote the
Philistines unto Gaza and the borders thereof, from the
tower of the watchmen to the fenced city.

xviii. 9-12.   *The fall of Samaria.*

9   And it came to pass in the fourth year of king Hezekiah, which was the seventh year of Hoshea son of Elah
king of Israel, that Shalmaneser king of Assyria came
10 up against Samaria, and besieged it.   And at the end of

---

burn incense : or rather 'sacrificed' (cf. xiv. 4).   The serpent-
idol had been retained in the Temple, where, though it may
officially have been regarded as the symbol of Jehovah, its
presence would inevitably lead to popular superstition.   It is
clear from this passage that serpent-worship continued in Israel
down to a comparatively late date.

and he called it Nehushtan : read with margin 'and it was
called' etc.   The name 'Nehushtan' is vocalized so as to suggest
in Hebrew the meaning 'piece of brass' (? a contemptuous
designation) ; but more probably it is connected with *naḥash*
(= 'serpent'), and refers to the primaeval serpent or serpent-
dragon.   If a contemptuous meaning is suggested this is due,
no doubt, to later feeling.

7.   he rebelled etc. : the statement implies that in this proceeding, also, Hezekiah 'prospered.'

8.   Hezekiah's Philistine campaign and re-conquest of Gaza
probably took place after the withdrawal of Sennacherib in
701 B.C.

from the tower etc. : cf. xvii. 9 and note.

9-12.   This passage embodies a notice, probably from the
Judaean annalistic document, of the fall of Samaria; *vv.* 9-11
are almost identical with xvii. 3-6.   The dates appear to be the
compiler's, and cannot be reconciled with *v.* 13 (see note there).

three years they took it: even in the sixth year of Hezekiah, which was the ninth year of Hoshea king of Israel, Samaria was taken. And the king of Assyria carried 11 Israel away unto Assyria, and put them in Halah, and in Habor, *on* the river of Gozan, and in the cities of the Medes: because they obeyed not the voice of the LORD 12 their God, but transgressed his covenant, even all that Moses the servant of the LORD commanded, and would not hear it, nor do it.

XVIII. 13-XIX. 37. SENNACHERIB'S CAMPAIGN.

(a) xviii. 13-16. *The annalistic account.*

Now in the fourteenth year of king Hezekiah did 13

xviii. 13-xix. 37. This passage, according to the opinion of recent critics, is made up of three independent narratives; (*a*) an annalistic account, inserted by the compiler (xviii. 13-16), and two narratives derived from the prophetical document, which may be called (*b*) the first prophetic narrative (xviii. 17-xix. 7 with 36, 37 as conclusion), and (*c*) the second prophetic narrative (xix. 8-35). The narratives (*b*) and (*c*) had already been combined in the prophetical document when the compiler used it as a source.

xviii. 13-16. This account undoubtedly is based upon the Judaean annalistic document. Two verses (=*vv.* 14-16) have been omitted (probably as without interest for the life of Isaiah) in the parallel text in Is. xxxvi. The passage agrees, on the whole, very closely with the account of the Assyrian campaign given in the inscriptions. According to the latter, Sennacherib's third campaign (in 701 B.C.) was directed against a confederacy of West Syrian States, which had been in rebellion since the death of Sargon (in 705 B.C.). Phoenicia was first reduced to submission; then the Philistine strongholds in the south were taken, and Judah under Hezekiah (who had led the confederacy) was dealt with last of all. The territory of Judah was devastated, forty-six fortresses were taken, and Jerusalem was blockaded, Hezekiah being shut up in his capital 'like a bird in a cage.' Hezekiah submitted, and paid as tribute 30 talents in gold and 800 in silver, this being sent after Sennacherib to Nineveh. Why he had returned to Nineveh is not stated. From the order of events as given in Sennacherib's inscription it may be inferred that Hezekiah's submission was only made after the defeat of the Egyptian forces at Eltekeh, which rendered all hope of assistance from that quarter vain.

13. in the fourteenth year etc.: this statement cannot be

Sennacherib king of Assyria come up against all the
14 fenced cities of Judah, and took them. And Hezekiah king
of Judah sent to the king of Assyria to Lachish, saying,
I have offended; return from me: that which thou puttest
on me will I bear. And the king of Assyria appointed
unto Hezekiah king of Judah three hundred talents of
15 silver and thirty talents of gold. And Hezekiah gave
him all the silver that was found in the house of the
16 LORD, and in the treasures of the king's house. At that
time did Hezekiah cut off *the gold from* the doors of the
temple of the LORD, and *from* the pillars which Hezekiah
king of Judah had overlaid, and gave it to the king of
Assyria.

(*b*) xviii. 17–xix. 7.   *The first prophetic narrative.*

17 And the king of Assyria sent Tartan and Rabsaris and
Rabshakeh from Lachish to king Hezekiah with a great

reconciled with xviii. 6, according to which Samaria was taken
(722 B.C.) in the sixth year of Hezekiah; 701 B.C. cannot, therefore, be Hezekiah's fourteenth year.   Perhaps 'in the fourteenth
year of Hezekiah' originally stood at the beginning of xx. 1, and
really marks the year of Hezekiah's sickness, which, if he came
to the throne in 720, would thus fall in 706 B.C.   The removal
of the date to its present position may be due to a later editor
who identified the year of the sickness with that of Sennacherib's
campaign.
   14.   to Lachish: an important Judaean stronghold on the
west; for its position, cf. xiv. 19 and note.
   three hundred talents of silver: according to the Assyrian
account it was 800 talents of silver.   The divergence has been
explained as due to 'the difference in weight between the Babylonian *light* and the Palestinian *heavy* talent.'
   xviii. 17–xix. 7.   Nothing corresponding to the incident here
described is recorded in the Assyrian account.   It may have taken
place after Hezekiah had already submitted, and the blockade of
Jerusalem had been raised.   The object of the demonstration of
force was to obtain possession of the city.
   17.   Tartan, or rather 'the Tartan,' was the title of the
Assyrian commander-in-chief, cf. Is. xx. 1; the other two names
('Rabshakeh' and 'Rabsaris') are also titles.   'Rabshakeh' (so
xix. 8) has been explained to mean 'chief of the officers.'   Is.
xxxvi. 2 names only the 'Rabshakeh.'

army unto Jerusalem. And they went up and came to
Jerusalem. And when they were come up, they came
and stood by the conduit of the upper pool, which is in
the high way of the fuller's field. And when they had 18
called to the king, there came out to them Eliakim the
son of Hilkiah, which was over the household, and
Shebnah the scribe, and Joah the son of Asaph the
recorder. And Rabshakeh said unto them, Say ye now 19
to Hezekiah, Thus saith the great king, the king of
Assyria, What confidence is this wherein thou trustest?
Thou sayest, but they are but vain words, *There is* 20
counsel and strength for the war. Now on whom dost
thou trust, that thou hast rebelled against me? Now, 21
behold, thou trustest upon the staff of this bruised reed,
even upon Egypt; whereon if a man lean, it will go into
his hand, and pierce it: so is Pharaoh king of Egypt
unto all that trust on him. But if ye say unto me, We 22
trust in the LORD our God: is not that he, whose high
places and whose altars Hezekiah hath taken away, and

---

the conduit etc. : cf. Is. vii. 3, and see note on xx. 20 below.
18. **Eliakim...Shebnah**: cf. Is. xxii. 15 f., where, however,
Shebna appears as 'over the household,' and it is prophesied
that Eliakim shall take his place. Apparently Eliakim's promotion to the higher office, and Shebna's vacation of it for the
lower one of 'scribe,' took place some time after the prophet
delivered his oracle, but before Sennacherib's invasion of 701.
The offices referred to are those of major-domo ('over the
household'), of secretary ('scribe'), whose business would be
to write documents, letters, records etc., and of recorder (lit.
'remembrancer'), whose duty was probably to bring important
matters to the king's notice ; cf. 1 Kings iv. 1 ff.
19. In this and the following verses the Rabshakeh attempts
to show how groundless is any hope, on the part of the Judaeans,
of help either from men or Jehovah. The speech, in its present
form, at any rate, must be regarded as a free composition by the
author of the narrative.
21. **staff...bruised reed** etc. : cf. Ezek. xxix. 6, 7, and illustrate
the general idea from Is. xxx. 1–5.
22. **whose high places** etc.: this implies that Hezekiah's
reforms had been carried out before 701 B.C. in the view of the

hath said to Judah and to Jerusalem, Ye shall worship
23 before this altar in Jerusalem? Now therefore, I pray
thee, give pledges to my master the king of Assyria, and
I will give thee two thousand horses, if thou be able on
24 thy part to set riders upon them. How then canst thou
turn away the face of one captain of the least of my
master's servants, and put thy trust on Egypt for chariots
25 and for horsemen? Am I now come up without the LORD
against this place to destroy it? The LORD said unto
26 me, Go up against this land, and destroy it. Then said
Eliakim the son of Hilkiah, and Shebnah, and Joah,
unto Rabshakeh, Speak, I pray thee, to thy servants in
the Syrian language; for we understand it: and speak
not with us in the Jews' language, in the ears of the
27 people that are on the wall. But Rabshakeh said unto
them, Hath my master sent me to thy master, and to
thee, to speak these words? *hath he* not *sent me* to the
men which sit on the wall, to eat their own dung, and to

---

author of this verse. But the verse may be a later addition; it
anticipates *v.* 30 in its reference to Jehovah, and interrupts the
address to Hezekiah in the second person.

23. give pledges to: or rather, as margin, 'make a wager
with.'

24. captain: the word means 'governor' (of a province), and
should probably be omitted as a gloss.

and put thy trust etc.: render as a fresh sentence: 'For
thou puttest thy trust in Egypt for chariots and horsemen!' For
Egypt as the source of supply for horses, cf. Is. xxxi. 1 and 3.
Deficiency in cavalry was a chronic difficulty in Judah.

25. without the Lord: i.e. without Jehovah's sanction. In
the same way Cyrus represented himself as the champion of the
incensed gods of Babylonia against Nabonidus, who had offended
conservative sentiment by reforms.

26. Syrian or 'Aramaic': Aramaic was the language of
diplomacy, and the medium of communication between educated
people of different nationalities in Western Asia; but among the
uneducated populace of Judah, Hebrew (called 'Jewish' in Neh.
xiii. 24) was still the vernacular.

27. to eat etc.: i.e. who, by their pitiable fidelity to a king
(Hezekiah) who can do nothing for them, will be forced to these
straits. This will be the inevitable result of such fatuous trust.

drink their own water with you? Then Rabshakeh stood, 28
and cried with a loud voice in the Jews' language, and
spake, saying, Hear ye the word of the great king, the
king of Assyria. Thus saith the king, Let not Hezekiah 29
deceive you; for he shall not be able to deliver you out
of his hand: neither let Hezekiah make you trust in the 30
LORD, saying, The LORD will surely deliver us, and this
city shall not be given into the hand of the king of
Assyria. Hearken not to Hezekiah: for thus saith the 31
king of Assyria, Make your peace with me, and come out
to me; and eat ye every one of his vine, and every one
of his fig tree, and drink ye every one the waters of his
own cistern; until I come and take you away to a land 32
like your own land, a land of corn and wine, a land of
bread and vineyards, a land of oil olive and of honey,
that ye may live, and not die: and hearken not unto
Hezekiah, when he persuadeth you, saying, The LORD
will deliver us. Hath any of the gods of the nations 33
ever delivered his land out of the hand of the king of
Assyria? Where are the gods of Hamath, and of Arpad? 34
where are the gods of Sepharvaim, of Hena, and Ivvah?

---

29. **out of his hand**: omit, in accordance with the parallel in
Isaiah (xxxvi. 14).

31. **Make your peace with me**: lit. 'make a blessing with
me,' i.e. prob. 'make a peaceful submission': the phrase is
peculiar.

come out to me: i.e. surrender the city; cf. Jer. xxi. 9 etc.

and eat ye: i.e. 'and ye shall eat' the produce of your own
fields and vineyards which you shall be able to cultivate in
peace.

32. **and take you away** etc.: i.e. by deportation.

32–35. **and hearken not** etc.: with this section cf. Is. x. 5–11.

34. For the cities here mentioned (with the exception of
Arpad) cf. xvii. 24 and note; Hamath was captured by Tiglath-
Pileser in 738, and again by Sargon in 720. If Sepharvaim =
Shabarain, this was destroyed by Shalmaneser IV. **Arpad** = the
modern *Tell-Erfâd*, about fifteen miles north of Aleppo: it was
captured by Tiglath-Pileser in 740.

35 have they delivered Samaria out of my hand? Who are
they among all the gods of the countries, that have
delivered their country out of my hand, that the LORD
36 should deliver Jerusalem out of my hand? But the people
held their peace, and answered him not a word: for the
king's commandment was, saying, Answer him not.
37 Then came Eliakim the son of Hilkiah, which was over
the household, and Shebna the scribe, and Joah the son
of Asaph the recorder, to Hezekiah with their clothes
rent, and told him the words of Rabshakeh.

19   And it came to pass, when king Hezekiah heard it,
that he rent his clothes, and covered himself with sack-
2 cloth, and went into the house of the LORD. And he
sent Eliakim, which was over the household, and Shebna
the scribe, and the elders of the priests, covered with
sackcloth, unto Isaiah the prophet the son of Amoz.
3 And they said unto him, Thus saith Hezekiah, This day
is a day of trouble, and of rebuke, and of contumely: for
the children are come to the birth, and there is not
4 strength to bring forth. It may be the LORD thy God
will hear all the words of Rabshakeh, whom the king of

---

have they delivered Samaria etc.: insert before this clause
with LXX (Luc.): 'Where are the gods of the land of Samaria?
Have they delivered' etc.

xix. 2. the elders of the priests: this implies that the priests
were already organized as a distinct corporation. This was, of
course, the case in the later period of the second Temple; cf.
Mishnah, *Yoma*, I. 5, where 'the elders of the priesthood' are
referred to.

unto Isaiah: Isaiah had consistently opposed the anti-Assyrian
party. Now the wisdom of the prophet's attitude is tacitly
acknowledged when his advice is sought by a deputation from
the king, which included Shebna whom he had bitterly denounced
(cf. Is. xxii. 15 f.).

3. of trouble...contumely: better 'of distress, and punishment, and rejection.'

the children are come etc.: for the figure (a proverbial one),
cf. Is. lxvi. 9. Here it expresses the king's conviction that the
limit of human resource has been reached.

Assyria his master hath sent to reproach the living God, and will rebuke the words which the LORD thy God hath heard: wherefore lift up thy prayer for the remnant that is left. So the servants of king Hezekiah came to Isaiah. 5 And Isaiah said unto them, Thus shall ye say to your 6 master, Thus saith the LORD, Be not afraid of the words that thou hast heard, wherewith the servants of the king of Assyria have blasphemed me. Behold, I will put a 7 spirit in him, and he shall hear a rumour, and shall return to his own land; and I will cause him to fall by the sword in his own land.

(c) xix. 8–35. *The second prophetic narrative.*

So Rabshakeh returned, and found the king of Assyria 8

---

4. thy God: the prophet stands in a nearer and more intimate relation to Jehovah than other men; hence his intercession will be more availing.

6. Thus saith the Lord etc.: the prophet has already received a revelation, dealing with the situation, from Jehovah.

7. a spirit in him: a spirit, namely, of fear: 'I will disquiet him.' This is explained in what follows.

he shall hear a rumour: probably tidings of revolt in Babylonia are referred to. The second narrative (cf. *v.* 9) connects the 'rumour' with the advance of Tirhakah.

8–35. The narrative that follows is to be regarded, according to the preponderating opinion of critical scholars, not as the sequel of what precedes, but as an independent account of what is described in xviii. 17–xix. 7. In other words it is a parallel account, based upon a different tradition, of the same events. Some scholars assign *vv.* 7–9 *a* to the first narrative, in which case the 'rumour' of *v.* 7 is explained by a supposed advance of Tirhakah, king of Ethiopia, against the Assyrians. But the activity of Tirhakah belongs to a period several years later than 701. The mention of Tirhakah, therefore, may be assigned more plausibly to the second narrative, which must be, in its present form, much later than the first. The main points in which the former differs from the latter are: (1) Sennacherib's demand takes the form of a threatening letter, which is despatched from Libnah, and conveyed by messengers unaccompanied by an army; (2) Isaiah's intervention is spontaneous—he sends a reassuring message to Hezekiah, without being appealed to (*v.* 20); (3) the cause assigned for the retreat of the Assyrian army is a

B.   8

warring against Libnah: for he had heard that he was
9 departed from Lachish. And when he heard say of
Tirhakah king of Ethiopia, Behold, he is come out to
fight against thee: he sent messengers again unto Heze-
10 kiah, saying, Thus shall ye speak to Hezekiah king of
Judah, saying, Let not thy God in whom thou trustest
deceive thee, saying, Jerusalem shall not be given into
11 the hand of the king of Assyria. Behold, thou hast
heard what the kings of Assyria have done to all lands,
by destroying them utterly: and shalt thou be delivered?
12 Have the gods of the nations delivered them, which my
fathers have destroyed, Gozan, and Haran, and Rezeph,
13 and the children of Eden which were in Telassar? Where

---

pestilence. It should be noticed that Isaiah's message to the
king, in the present form of the text, consists of two distinct
oracles. One of these is a metrical composition (*vv.* 21-28) with
a prose appendix (*vv.* 29-31), and was probably inserted in the
text of the narrative after the original composition of the latter,
from another source. The actual oracle of Isaiah, in answer to
Hezekiah's prayer, is contained in *vv.* 32-34, which, doubtless,
originally followed *v.* 20 immediately. The two narratives have
been connected together by *v.* 8.

8. Libnah: cf. viii. 22 and note. The verse implies that
Lachish had capitulated during the interval of the Rabshakeh's
absence. The detail may be an inference on the part of the
compiler who joined the two narratives together.

9. Tirhakah did not become supreme in Egypt, apparently,
till 691. One or two scholars, therefore, think that this narrative
refers to a later expedition of Sennacherib against Jerusalem
than that of 701; but nothing is known of such an expedition.

sent messengers again: 'again' is probably an editorial
addition. Is. xxxvii. 9 has a different word.

10. Thus shall ye speak…saying: the clause is omitted by
the LXX. With this omission *vv.* 10-13 may be regarded as
giving the substance of the letter. Otherwise they give an oral
message which the messengers delivered with the letter. The
verses repeat the arguments of xviii. 29-35.

12, 13. The greater number of the places here mentioned
have already been referred to (cf. xvii. 6, 24; xviii. 33 f.).
Haran (cf. Gen. xi. 31)=the *Carrhae* of the Romans, was an
important commercial town in north-west Mesopotamia; **Rezeph**
(Assyrian *Raṣṣappa*), the modern *Ruṣâfe*, is south of the Euphrates

is the king of Hamath, and the king of Arpad, and the
king of the city of Sepharvaim, of Hena, and Ivvah?
And Hezekiah received the letter from the hand of the 14
messengers, and read it : and Hezekiah went up unto
the house of the LORD, and spread it before the LORD.
And Hezekiah prayed before the LORD, and said, O LORD, 15
the God of Israel, that sittest upon the cherubim, thou
art the God, even thou alone, of all the kingdoms of the
earth ; thou hast made heaven and earth.   Incline thine 16
ear, O LORD, and hear ; open thine eyes, O LORD, and
see : and hear the words of Sennacherib, wherewith he
hath sent him to reproach the living God.   Of a truth, 17
LORD, the kings of Assyria have laid waste the nations
and their lands, and have cast their gods into the fire : 18
for they were no gods, but the work of men's hands,
wood and stone; therefore they have destroyed them.
Now therefore, O LORD our God, save thou us, I be- 19
seech thee, out of his hand, that all the kingdoms of the
earth may know that thou art the LORD God, even thou
only.

---

and north of Palmyra, on the road to which city it lies; **Eden**
is the Assyrian *Bit Adini*, a small kingdom on the upper
Euphrates ;   probably **Telassar** = *Til-Bashir*, one of its important cities.   All these provinces had for centuries formed
part of the Assyrian Empire.

15. **that sittest upon the cherubim** : or rather 'who art
enthroned upon the cherubim.'   By the 'cherubim' here are
meant the two figures over the ark in the innermost sanctuary
of the Temple; cf. 1 Sam. iv. 4; 2 Sam. vi. 2 etc.   The phrase,
as here used, contains an implicit appeal to the reality of the
divine presence in the sanctuary.

16. **sent him** : omit 'him' with the LXX and Is. xxxvii. 17.

17. **have laid waste** : read rather 'have devoted them' (the
same word as in *v.* 11 ; cf. margin there).

18. **wood and stone** : this description of heathen gods is
emphasized especially in the latter part of the Book of Isaiah
(cf. Is. xl. 19, xli. 6 f., xliv. 13 f.; cf. also Deut. iv. 28 etc.).

19. **that thou art the Lord...only** : or better 'that thou,
Jehovah, art God alone'—the true God, in contrast to the dead
idols.

20   Then Isaiah the son of Amoz sent to Hezekiah, saying, Thus saith the LORD, the God of Israel, Whereas thou hast prayed to me against Sennacherib king of Assyria,

21 I have heard *thee*. This is the word that the LORD hath spoken concerning him: The virgin daughter of Zion hath despised thee and laughed thee to scorn; the daughter of Jerusalem hath shaken her head at thee.

22 Whom hast thou reproached and blasphemed? and against whom hast thou exalted thy voice and lifted up thine eyes on high? *even* against the Holy One of Israel.

23 By thy messengers thou hast reproached the Lord, and hast said, With the multitude of my chariots am I come up to the height of the mountains, to the innermost parts of Lebanon; and I will cut down the tall cedars thereof, and the choice fir trees thereof: and I will enter into his

24 farthest lodging place, the forest of his fruitful field. I have digged and drunk strange waters, and with the sole

---

20. This verse containing the prophet's message, which forms the answer to Hezekiah's prayer, was, in the original form of the text, the protasis to *v.* 32 (the words **I have heard thee** are omitted in Isaiah): 'whereas thou hast prayed to me etc. therefore thus saith the Lord' etc.

21–28 (29–31). The poem, with prose appendix, which is contained in these verses is a taunt-song upon the defeat of Sennacherib and the Assyrian army. The poem is in the so-called 'qinah' or elegiac rhythm, consisting of long lines followed by short. Thus the opening lines in *v.* 21 may be represented as follows:

> *Thee, thee she despises, she scorns—*
> > *Zion, the virgin-daughter!*
> *Behind thee she shakes her head—*
> > *the virgin Jerusalem!*

21. hath shaken her head: a gesture marking derision; cf. Ps. xxii. 7; Lam. ii. 15 etc.

23. With...my chariots etc.: the most inaccessible places have been reached by the Assyrian engines of war—a common Assyrian boast. 'I will cut down' and 'I will enter' should be rendered rather 'I have cut down,' 'I have entered.'

the forest of his fruitful field: lit. 'its forest-garden,' i.e. its thickest woods.

of my feet will I dry up all the rivers of Egypt. Hast 25
thou not heard how I have done it long ago, and formed
it of ancient times? now have I brought it to pass, that
thou shouldest be to lay waste fenced cities into ruinous
heaps. Therefore their inhabitants were of small power, 26
they were dismayed and confounded; they were as the
grass of the field, and as the green herb, as the grass on
the housetops, and as corn blasted before it be grown
up. But I know thy sitting down, and thy going out, 27
and thy coming in, and thy raging against me. Because 28
of thy raging against me, and for that thine arrogancy is
come up into mine ears, therefore will I put my hook in
thy nose, and my bridle in thy lips, and I will turn thee
back by the way by which thou camest. And this shall 29
be the sign unto thee: ye shall eat this year that which

---

24. the rivers of Egypt: R.V. marg. has 'defence' for
'Egypt,' incorrectly. No Assyrian army entered Egypt till long
after 701 B.C.

25. Here follows the divine reply, Jehovah being the speaker.
The Assyrian, though he knows it not, is simply the instrument
for carrying out Jehovah's purposes, which have been planned
long ago. For the thought cf. Is. x. 6 f., xlv. 1 f. The opening
clauses of the verse should, perhaps, be transposed:

'Long ago I have done (prepared) it—hast thou not heard?'

26. grass on the housetops: cf. Ps. cxxix. 6–8.

corn blasted...grown up: the Heb. text here is corrupt and
yields no sense. Perhaps the text should be emended so as to
read one word at the end of *v.* 26 ('hills'); and then continue
(*v.* 27): 'Before me (is) thy rising up' etc. (omitting 'but I
know').

27, 28. and thy raging...arrogancy: there is an awkward
repetition in the text: read 'Thy raging and uproar against
me.'

28. my hook in thy nose: cf. Ezek. xix. 4, xxix. 4, xxxviii.
4. The Assyrian is compared to a wild animal, which is con-
trolled by a nose-ring, reins and bridle.

the way...thou camest: cf. *v.* 33.

29–31. These verses form a prose appendix.

29. the sign here described is not any striking or supernatural
manifestation, but a perfectly natural series of events, the sequence
of which is foreseen by the prophet. After they have happened

groweth of itself, and in the second year that which springeth of the same; and in the third year sow ye, and reap, and plant vineyards, and eat the fruit thereof.

30 And the remnant that is escaped of the house of Judah shall again take root downward, and bear fruit upward.

31 For out of Jerusalem shall go forth a remnant, and out of mount Zion they that shall escape: the zeal of the

32 LORD shall perform this. Therefore thus saith the LORD concerning the king of Assyria, He shall not come unto this city, nor shoot an arrow there, neither shall he come

33 before it with shield, nor cast a mount against it. By the way that he came, by the same shall he return, and

34 he shall not come unto this city, saith the LORD. For I will defend this city to save it, for mine own sake, and for my servant David's sake.

35   And it came to pass that night, that the angel of the

---

as described they will serve as a proof and reminder of the truth of the prophet's words. The announcement is that the regular harvest for the year when the prediction is uttered (in the summer of 701) will have been destroyed (by the Assyrian invaders, before it could be reaped); in consequence the people will have to depend upon 'that which groweth of itself' (from the shaken ears of corn; cf. Lev. xxv. 5, 11); in the next year (from the autumn of 701 to autumn 700), on 'that which springeth up from it,' i.e. grain that shoots up of itself (no regular ploughing or sowing having taken place in the autumn of 701); only in the third year (summer of 699) will the usual harvest, after sowing and ploughing, be resumed. The old Hebrew year began in the autumn.

32. Therefore: here the original oracle of Isaiah, as it at first stood in the narrative, is introduced. 'Therefore' resumes 'whereas' in *v.* 20.

33. By the way etc.: cf. *v.* 28. Isaiah's oracle gives no hint of the destruction of the Assyrian army by pestilence as described in *v.* 35.

35. the angel of the Lord (here probably distinguished from Jehovah as a creature angel; contrast i. 3): cf. 2 Sam. xxiv. 15, where 'the angel of the Lord' is similarly associated with pestilence. By 'that night' must be meant the night of the pestilence. An Egyptian legend, recorded by Herodotus, states that an

LORD went forth, and smote in the camp of the Assyrians an hundred fourscore and five thousand: and when men arose early in the morning, behold, they were all dead corpses.

xix. 36, 37. *Conclusion of the first prophetic narrative.*

So Sennacherib king of Assyria departed, and went 36 and returned, and dwelt at Nineveh. And it came to 37 pass, as he was worshipping in the house of Nisroch his god, that Adrammelech and Sharezer smote him with the sword: and they escaped into the land of Ararat. And Esar-haddon his son reigned in his stead.

Assyrian invasion of Egypt under Sennacherib was prevented by field-mice gnawing the bows of the soldiers, and the thongs of their shields ('field-mice' were a symbol of pestilence). It appears from the inscriptions that Sennacherib after 690 B.C. undertook an expedition against the Arabians. Winckler supposes that further operations were contemplated in this campaign, against Egypt which was now ruled by Tirhakah, and that the second prophetic narrative refers to incidents of his time. The threatened invasion of Egypt was frustrated by a pestilence among the Assyrian troops (cf. Herodotus II. 141).

36, 37. These verses may be regarded as the conclusion of the first narrative (resuming *v.* 7), though they form an equally appropriate ending to the second.

37. Nisroch: no god of this name can be identified; perhaps 'Nisroch' is a corrupt form of *Nusku*, a solar deity sometimes mentioned in the inscriptions.

Adrammelech and Sharezer: Adrammelech is mentioned elsewhere as the murderer of Sennacherib (in 681 B.C.). *Sharezer* is not otherwise known (unless, as Ball suggests, the name should be combined with 'Nergilos' [=Nergal-Sharezer] referred to in Abydenus [*ap.* Eusebius] as slain by Esarhaddon); cf. Jer. xxxix. 3.

the land of Ararat = Armenia. Esarhaddon reigned 681–668.

xx. 1–11. There is no doubt that the two episodes described in xx. 1–19 precede chronologically the events described in the previous chapters; they must have taken place before the Assyrian campaign of 701. A compiler, however, seems to have placed them wrongly in this year; hence the insertion of *v.* 6, which probably does not belong to the original form of the narrative. In the parallel passage in Is. xxxviii., the so-called

XX. 1-11. HEZEKIAH'S ILLNESS AND RECOVERY
(= Is. xxxviii. 1-8, 21, 22).

20 In those days was Hezekiah sick unto death. And
Isaiah the prophet the son of Amoz came to him, and
said unto him, Thus saith the LORD, Set thine house in
2 order; for thou shalt die, and not live. Then he turned
his face to the wall, and prayed unto the LORD, saying,
3 Remember now, O LORD, I beseech thee, how I have
walked before thee in truth and with a perfect heart,
and have done that which is good in thy sight. And
4 Hezekiah wept sore. And it came to pass, afore Isaiah
was gone out into the middle part of the city, that the
5 word of the LORD came to him, saying, Turn again, and
say to Hezekiah the prince of my people, Thus saith the
LORD, the God of David thy father, I have heard thy
prayer, I have seen thy tears: behold, I will heal thee:
on the third day thou shalt go up unto the house of the
6 LORD. And I will add unto thy days fifteen years; and
I will deliver thee and this city out of the hand of the
king of Assyria; and I will defend this city for mine own
7 sake, and for my servant David's sake. And Isaiah

'Psalm of Hezekiah' has been inserted (Is. xxxviii. 9-20), and
there are other variations in the text.

1. In those days: some scholars think that the *datum* 'in
the fourteenth year of king Hezekiah' (xviii. 13) originally stood
at the head of this chapter, which preceded xviii. 13 ff.

Set thine house in order: 'give (the last) directions to thy
household': cf. 1 Kings ii. 1-9; 2 Sam. xvii. 23.

2. turned his face: cf. 1 Kings xxi. 4.

4. into the middle etc.: read with margin 'of the middle
court,' i.e. the court in which the palace stood, adjoining the
Temple; cf. 1 Kings viii. 7. Isaiah had not left the palace
precincts before he was bidden to return.

5. prince of my people: cf. 1 Kings i. 35 (1 Sam. x. 1 etc.).

6. fifteen years: this agrees with xviii. 2 and 13.

and I will deliver...sake: this clause has every appearance of
being an insertion; the logical connexion with *v.* 7 is much
improved by its omission.

said, Take a cake of figs. And they took and laid it on
the boil, and he recovered. And Hezekiah said unto 8
Isaiah, What shall be the sign that the LORD will heal
me, and that I shall go up unto the house of the LORD
the third day? And Isaiah said, This shall be the sign 9
unto thee from the LORD, that the LORD will do the
thing that he hath spoken: shall the shadow go forward
ten steps, or go back ten steps? And Hezekiah answered, 10
It is a light thing for the shadow to decline ten steps:
nay, but let the shadow return backward ten steps. And 11
Isaiah the prophet cried unto the LORD: and he brought
the shadow ten steps backward, by which it had gone
down on the dial of Ahaz.

7. Take a cake of figs: i.e. figs pressed into a cake (cf. 1 Sam.
xxv. 18). The medicinal use of figs, which is still not uncommon
in the East, is of great antiquity.

the boil: i.e. an ulcer of some kind; cf. Ex. ix. 9; Job ii. 7.
It was not a case of pestilence.

8. What shall be the sign etc.: both this verse and *v.* 7
have apparently been added from Kings to the chapter in
Isaiah, which contains the parallel account, but at the end
(Is. xxxviii. 21, 22). The addition may have been originally
a marginal gloss. In the original Isaiah narrative (xxxviii. 1–8)
the sign is voluntarily given by the prophet, without any question
by Hezekiah.

9. shall the shadow etc.: read, as in the margin, 'The
shadow is gone forward ten steps.'

or go back ten steps? By a slight emendation the text will
read, 'it shall go back ten steps.' As in Is. xxxviii. 8 the
prophet simply announces the sign; he does not offer Hezekiah
an alternative.

10. This verse looks like a later expansion, suggested by the
modification introduced into the previous verse. There is nothing
corresponding to it in Isaiah xxxviii.

decline: or 'go forward' (*v.* 9). The same word is used in
the Hebrew in both cases. The shadow normally extended
down the steps, with the progress of the sun. Its sudden retro-
gression would therefore appear all the more marvellous.

11. by which it had gone down: in Is. xxxviii. 8 the subject
of this sentence is the sun.

the dial of Ahaz: or 'the steps of Ahaz' (marg.). A simple
flight of steps, which served the purposes of a sun-dial, is apparently meant (not a regularly constructed sun-dial).

XX. 12–19. The embassy of Merodach-Baladan
(= Is. xxxix.).

12 At that time Berodach-baladan the son of Baladan,
king of Babylon, sent letters and a present unto Hezekiah: for he had heard that Hezekiah had been sick.
13 And Hezekiah hearkened unto them, and shewed them
all the house of his precious things, the silver, and the
gold, and the spices, and the precious oil, and the house
of his armour, and all that was found in his treasures:
there was nothing in his house, nor in all his dominion,
14 that Hezekiah shewed them not.   Then came Isaiah the
prophet unto king Hezekiah, and said unto him, What

12–19. Merodach-Baladan is often mentioned in Assyrian
inscriptions during the reigns of Tiglath-Pileser, Shalmaneser, Sargon, and Sennacherib.   He was the ruler of
Bit-Yakin, a small Chaldean state at the head of the Persian
Gulf.   He was often in conflict with the Assyrian kings, and
established himself in a semi-independent position as king of
Babylon at the beginning of Sargon's reign (721), reigning till
710, when he was defeated by Sargon.   At the beginning of
Sennacherib's reign (perhaps 705–704) he again rebelled, and
reigned in Babylon independently for nine months.   The embassy
here referred to may have taken place about 705, following
Hezekiah's sickness in 706.   Under pretext of congratulating
Hezekiah on his recovery the Chaldean monarch apparently
suggested an anti-Assyrian alliance.   Some scholars favour an
earlier date.

12. Berodach-baladan: read 'Merodach-Baladan' (the Heb.
form of Marduk-apal-iddin) as in Is. xxxix. 1 (so LXX).

had been sick : add with Is. xxxix. 1 'and had recovered.'

13. hearkened unto them : a scribal error; read 'and was
glad because of them' (so Is. xxxix. 2 and some MSS with the
Versions here).

the house of his precious things : the Hebrew expression
here, which is unusual, = the Assyrian *bit nakamti*, i.e. ' treasure-
house,' and so the Targum, Syr. and LXX (Luc.) render.   The
treasures of an Oriental king would include not only **silver** and
gold, but also **spices** and **oil** (i.e. fine oil used for anointing) ;
cf. 1 Kings x. 10.

the house of his armour : i.e. the royal armoury, which was
probably identical with the 'House of the Forest of Lebanon'
(cf. 1 Kings vii. 2 f. ; Is. xxii. 8).

said these men? and from whence came they unto thee?
And Hezekiah said, They are come from a far country,
even from Babylon. And he said, What have they seen 15
in thine house? And Hezekiah answered, All that is in
mine house have they seen : there is nothing among my
treasures that I have not shewed them. And Isaiah said 16
unto Hezekiah, Hear the word of the LORD. Behold, the 17
days come, that all that is in thine house, and that which
thy fathers have laid up in store unto this day, shall be
carried to Babylon : nothing shall be left, saith the LORD.
And of thy sons that shall issue from thee, which thou 18
shalt beget, shall they take away ; and they shall be
eunuchs in the palace of the king of Babylon. Then 19
said Hezekiah unto Isaiah, Good is the word of the
LORD which thou hast spoken. He said moreover, Is
it not so, if peace and truth shall be in my days?

xx. **20, 21.** *Concluding notice of Hezekiah's reign.*

Now the rest of the acts of Hezekiah, and all his might, 20
and how he made the pool, and the conduit, and brought

17, 18. In its present form the language of these verses—
which obviously refer to the Babylonian captivity—seems to be
coloured by later events. The verses reflect the later feeling
about Babylon, when it had changed places with Assyria and
become the oppressive world-power.

18. thy sons : i.e. thy descendants.

19. Good is the word of the Lord : Hezekiah expresses pious
acquiescence in God's will ; cf. 1 Sam. iii. 18 (Eli).

peace and truth : or rather ' peace and stability ' (i.e. settled
rule). Hezekiah solaces himself with the thought that these
blessings are assured to him during his own life-time. This clause
is lacking in the LXX.

20. the pool, and the conduit etc. : cf. the amplified notice
in 2 Chron. xxxii. 30. An ancient tunnel exists connecting the
Pool of Siloam (below the inner side of the Temple hill) with
the so-called ' Virgin's Spring ' (the only natural spring near
Jerusalem), which rises below the walls of the city on the
western bank of the Kidron valley. In this way the waters of
the spring would be made available in case of siege. No doubt
this is the work to which reference is made in our text. Cf. also
Ecclus. xlviii. 17.

water into the city, are they not written in the book of
21 the chronicles of the kings of Judah? And Hezekiah
slept with his fathers: and Manasseh his son reigned in
his stead.

XXI. 1–18. MANASSEH OF JUDAH (cf. 2 Chron.
xxxiii. 1–20).

xxi. 1, 2. *Introduction.*

21 Manasseh was twelve years old when he began to
reign; and he reigned five and fifty years in Jerusalem:
2 and his mother's name was Hephzi-bah. And he did
that which was evil in the sight of the LORD, after the
abominations of the heathen, whom the LORD cast out
before the children of Israel.

xxi. 3–16. *Manasseh's evil reign.*

3 For he built again the high places which Hezekiah his
father had destroyed; and he reared up altars for Baal,

---

xxi. 1–18. The long reign of Manasseh (55 years) marks a period
of reaction against the higher prophetic religion. The prophetic
party, which had been powerful in the reign of Hezekiah, and
had inspired that monarch's reforming measures, was fiercely
persecuted (cf. *v.* 16), and heathenism in all its forms and
practices revived. Later times looked back upon this period as
the culmination of national apostasy (cf. xxiii. 26). The present
section appears to be wholly the work of one or other of the
redactors of Kings, no excerpt from older sources having been
embodied. In *vv.* 7–15 the Exile is presupposed, and these
verses were probably inserted by the later (exilic) redactor.
Manasseh's reign is, in the main, parallel with those of the
Assyrian kings Esar-haddon (681–668) and Asshur-bani-pal
(668–626), during which the conquest of Egypt was effected (in
670 and following years). According to 2 Chron. xxxiii. 11–13
Manasseh was carried a captive to Babylon, at that time a seat
of the Assyrian court (probably for participation in a revolt
against Asshur-bani-pal in 647 B.C.).

xxi. 1. Hephzi-bah: cf. Is. lxii. 4 (a poetical name of Sion).

2. did that which was evil etc.: the sins referred to are the
introduction or revival of various forms of heathen worship, as
described in the following verses.

3. the high places...Hezekiah ... had destroyed: for
Hezekiah's reformation see xviii. 4 and notes.

and made an Asherah, as did Ahab king of Israel, and
worshipped all the host of heaven, and served them.
And he built altars in the house of the LORD, whereof 4
the LORD said, In Jerusalem will I put my name. And 5
he built altars for all the host of heaven in the two courts
of the house of the LORD. And he made his son to pass 6
through the fire, and practised augury, and used enchantments, and dealt with them that had familiar spirits,
and with wizards: he wrought much evil in the sight of
the LORD, to provoke him to anger. And he set the 7
graven image of Asherah, that he had made, in the
house of which the LORD said to David and to Solomon
his son, In this house, and in Jerusalem, which I have
chosen out of all the tribes of Israel, will I put my name
for ever: neither will I cause the feet of Israel to wander 8

---

an Asherah: cf. xiii. 6 and note.

as did Ahab: see 1 Kings xvi. 32, 33.

all the host of heaven: Babylonian star-worship (worship of
sun, moon and stars) had been introduced by Ahaz (cf. xvii. 16),
and was very prevalent in Judah in the 7th century B.C. and
down to the Exile (cf. Deut. iv. 19, xvii. 3; Jer. viii. 2, xix.
13 etc.).

4. altars: i.e. idolatrous altars.

In Jerusalem...name: cf. 1 Kings viii. 16, x. 3 (referring to
the building of the Temple).

5. in the two courts etc.: possibly the palace-court is
included. The pre-exilic Temple proper apparently possessed
only one court (cf. 1 Kings vi. 36).

6. On child-sacrifice cf. xvi. 3 and note. **Augury** and
enchantment are strictly forbidden in Deut. xviii. 10, 11, as well
as dealings with **them that had familiar spirits and with
wizards**.

7. the graven image of Asherah: this seems to be a clear
case of 'Asherah' being used as the name of a goddess; cf. xiii. 6
and note.

the Lord said etc.: cf. 1 Kings viii. 15–26, ix. 1 f. The
climax of Manasseh's iniquity was reached when he set up the
Asherah-image in the sanctuary itself.

8. neither will I cause etc.: Israel's freedom from the doom
of exile is conditional on obedience to the divine requirements.
This passage was probably written after the Babylonian Exile
had taken place.

any more out of the land which I gave their fathers; if only they will observe to do according to all that I have commanded them, and according to all the law that my

9 servant Moses commanded them. But they hearkened not: and Manasseh seduced them to do that which is evil more than did the nations, whom the LORD destroyed

10 before the children of Israel. And the LORD spake by

11 his servants the prophets, saying, Because Manasseh king of Judah hath done these abominations, and hath done wickedly above all that the Amorites did, which were before him, and hath made Judah also to sin

12 with his idols: therefore thus saith the LORD, the God of Israel, Behold, I bring such evil upon Jerusalem and Judah, that whosoever heareth of it, both his ears shall

13 tingle. And I will stretch over Jerusalem the line of Samaria, and the plummet of the house of Ahab: and I will wipe Jerusalem as a man wipeth a dish, wiping it

14 and turning it upside down. And I will cast off the remnant of mine inheritance, and deliver them into the hand of their enemies; and they shall become a prey

15 and a spoil to all their enemies; because they have done

---

9. evil: add (with LXX) 'in the eyes of the Lord' (as in *vv.* 2, 15 etc.).

10. by his servants the prophets: the prophetic protests are summarized in *vv.* 11-15. Probably members of the prophetic party (especially Isaiah's disciples) are referred to, whose names have not come down to us.

12. both his ears shall tingle: cf. 1 Sam. iii. 11; Jer. xix. 3.

13. I will stretch over Jerusalem etc.: cf. Amos vii. 7-9; Is. xxxiv. 11; Lam. ii. 8. The meaning is 'I will mete out to Jerusalem the fate of Samaria, and the destiny of the house of Ahab to its dynasty.' Plummet and line were necessary adjuncts for determining the plan of a building, and hence come to symbolize 'fate' or 'destiny' generally (not necessarily destruction).

as a man wipeth a dish etc.: a strong simile for utter destruction ('wiping out'). Cf. Is. xxiv. 1 (emptying the earth and turning it upside down).

that which is evil in my sight, and have provoked me to anger, since the day their fathers came forth out of Egypt, even unto this day. Moreover Manasseh shed 16 innocent blood very much, till he had filled Jerusalem from one end to another; beside his sin wherewith he made Judah to sin, in doing that which was evil in the sight of the LORD.

xxi. 17, 18. *Conclusion.*

Now the rest of the acts of Manasseh, and all that he 17 did, and his sin that he sinned, are they not written in the book of the chronicles of the kings of Judah? And 18 Manasseh slept with his fathers, and was buried in the garden of his own house, in the garden of Uzza: and Amon his son reigned in his stead.

XXI. 19–26. AMON OF JUDAH (cf. 2 Chron. xxxiii. 21–25).
xxi. 19–22. *Introduction.*

Amon was twenty and two years old when he began 19 to reign; and he reigned two years in Jerusalem: and his mother's name was Meshullemeth the daughter of Haruz of Jotbah. And he did that which was evil in 20 the sight of the LORD, as did Manasseh his father. And 21 he walked in all the way that his father walked in, and served the idols that his father served, and worshipped them: and he forsook the LORD, the God of his fathers, 22 and walked not in the way of the LORD.

---

16. The narrative is resumed from *v.* 9. The verse apparently alludes to a bloody persecution of the prophetic party. According to later tradition the prophet Isaiah was among the victims, being sawn asunder.

18. in the garden of Uzza: 'Uzza' is prob. a corruption of Uzziah (= Azariah). This garden may have been one laid out by Uzziah in close proximity to the royal palace (and the Temple; cf. Ezek. xliii. 7). Here Amon was also buried (*v.* 26). After Hezekiah no king seems to have been buried in the ancient sepulchres of the kings of Judah in the city of David.

19. Jotbah: according to Jerome the name of a town in Judah (otherwise unknown).

xxi. 23, 24. Murder of Amon.

23 And the servants of Amon conspired against him, and
24 put the king to death in his own house. But the people
of the land slew all them that had conspired against
king Amon; and the people of the land made Josiah
his son king in his stead.

xxi. 25, 26. Conclusion.

25 Now the rest of the acts of Amon which he did, are they
not written in the book of the chronicles of the kings of
26 Judah? And he was buried in his sepulchre in the
garden of Uzza: and Josiah his son reigned in his stead.

XXII. 1–XXIII. 30. JOSIAH OF JUDAH (cf. 2 Chron.
xxxiv. 1–xxxv. 27).

xxii. 1, 2. Introduction.

22   Josiah was eight years old when he began to reign;
and he reigned thirty and one years in Jerusalem: and

23, 24. This notice is probably dependent upon the chronicles
of Judah. The courtiers who murdered the king did not have
popular opinion behind them. By 'the people of the land' is
probably meant the populace generally, both in Jerusalem and
outside, as opposed to the palace officials.

26. in his sepulchre: LXX (Luc.) 'in the sepulchre of his
father.'

xxii. 1–xxiii. 30. The long section that is devoted to the
reign of Josiah is mainly occupied with an account of the
discovery in the Temple of the Law-Book, and the reformation
of the cultus that followed.

That the Law-Book found in the Temple was some form of
our present Book of Deuteronomy is generally admitted. The
reforms actually carried out correspond to injunctions found in
that book (see notes below) and some of them in that book only.
As it was read through, publicly twice in the same day, the code
could not have been of any great length, and indeed was probably
shorter than Deuteronomy in its present form.

No information is given as to the time of composition and
authorship of the Code. But that it was really discovered in the
Temple need not seriously be doubted. It may have been

his mother's name was Jedidah the daughter of Adaiah
of Bozkath. And he did that which was right in the 2
eyes of the LORD, and walked in all the way of David
his father, and turned not aside to the right hand or to
the left.

xxii. 3–20. *The discovery of the Law-book.*

And it came to pass in the eighteenth year of king 3
Josiah, that the king sent Shaphan the son of Azaliah,
the son of Meshullam, the scribe, to the house of the
LORD, saying, Go up to Hilkiah the high priest, that he 4
may sum the money which is brought into the house of
the LORD, which the keepers of the door have gathered
of the people: and let them deliver it into the hand of 5
the workmen that have the oversight of the house of the

---

written and stored away during the dark days of Manasseh.
The central part of the present section (apart from the Introduction and Conclusion) is probably based on the Temple-
history which we have already met with as one of the sources of
our book (see introduction to xii. 4–16). Into this source some
glosses and one or two Deuteronomic and later insertions (e.g.
xxii. 16–20, xxiii. 16–20, 25, 26–27) appear to have been introduced. But the older stratum substantially remains intact, and
as it must have been older than both Deuteronomic redactors,
is an authority of the highest value, almost contemporary with
the events here described.

xxii. 1. Bozkath: a town in the lowland of Judah (Josh. xv.
39), otherwise unknown.

3–20. The visit of Shaphan, the king's secretary, to the
Temple took place in connexion with the distribution of the
funds collected for the repair of the Temple fabric (cf. xii. 9 f.).
It is on this occasion that the priest Hilkiah produces the Law-
Book which he has discovered. It is read to the king, and the
prophetess Huldah is consulted. The 18th year of Josiah=621
B.C.

4. the high priest: in *vv.* 10, 12, 14 and xxiii. 24 Hilkiah
is described as 'the priest' only; prob. 'high' is a later addition
here, and in *v.* 8; cf. xii. 10 and xxiii. 4. The office of 'high-
priest' was a post-exilic institution.

sum: i.e. make up the amount of; LXX (B) has 'seal up,'
which represents a better reading of the Hebrew text.

5–7. Cf. notes on xii. 9 f.

LORD: and let them give it to the workmen which are
in the house of the LORD, to repair the breaches of the
6 house; unto the carpenters, and to the builders, and to
the masons; and for buying timber and hewn stone to
7 repair the house. Howbeit there was no reckoning made
with them of the money that was delivered into their
8 hand; for they dealt faithfully. And Hilkiah the high
priest said unto Shaphan the scribe, I have found the
book of the law in the house of the LORD. And Hilkiah
9 delivered the book to Shaphan, and he read it. And
Shaphan the scribe came to the king, and brought the
king word again, and said, Thy servants have emptied
out the money that was found in the house, and have
delivered it into the hand of the workmen that have the
10 oversight of the house of the LORD. And Shaphan the
scribe told the king, saying, Hilkiah the priest hath
delivered me a book. And Shaphan read it before the
11 king. And it came to pass, when the king had heard
the words of the book of the law, that he rent his clothes.
12 And the king commanded Hilkiah the priest, and

---

8. the book of the law: this rendering is, perhaps, to be
preferred to the indefinite 'a book of the law.' In the mouth of
Hilkiah the expression would suggest the discovery of an old
(and well-known) code, which had been lost. On the hypothesis
that the law-book had lain hidden and forgotten in the Temple,
since some time in the reign of Manasseh, this is possible. But
it seems more probable that the expression represents the view
of the writer of the source, to whom Deuteronomy had become
'the book of the law' *par excellence*. In *v.* 10 the indefinite
expression 'a book' is used by Shaphan.

10. read it: i.e. read it right through. To the Chronicler
'the book of the law' could only mean the whole Pentateuch;
hence he has altered the expression here to 'read *therein*'
(2 Chron. xxxiv. 18).

11. What seems to have impressed the king most deeply were
the threats of punishment for disobedience contained in Deut.
xxviii., xxix. (cf. *vv.* 13, 16, 17). This would form the concluding section of the 'law-book.'

12–20. The king's desire for prophetic guidance in the crisis
may be explained by his resolve to undo, as far as possible, the

Ahikam the son of Shaphan, and Achbor the son of
Micaiah, and Shaphan the scribe, and Asaiah the king's
servant, saying, Go ye, inquire of the LORD for me, and for 13
the people, and for all Judah, concerning the words of
this book that is found : for great is the wrath of the LORD
that is kindled against us, because our fathers have not
hearkened unto the words of this book, to do according
unto all that which is written concerning us.   So Hilkiah 14
the priest, and Ahikam, and Achbor, and Shaphan, and
Asaiah, went unto Huldah the prophetess, the wife of
Shallum the son of Tikvah, the son of Harhas, keeper
of the wardrobe; (now she dwelt in Jerusalem in the
second quarter;) and they communed with her.   And 15

---

evil consequences to the nation of past neglect of the divine law.
The oracle which the prophetess Huldah delivers in response to
the royal enquiry (*vv.* 16–20) is, in its present form, an un-
compromising prophecy of doom upon the nation.   Many critics
think this is hard to reconcile with the zeal with which Josiah
immediately undertook the task of reform.   If reform was thus
declared to be hopeless, how could it have been taken in hand
with such enthusiasm ?   Possibly in its original form the oracle
was much less gloomy, and, perhaps, contained an element of
promise for obedience.   The heightened gloom may be due to a
later time (period of the Exile), when events had demonstrated
how ineffectual reform really was to save the national polity.
The last part of the oracle (*vv.* 19, 20) cannot, however, have
been composed after Josiah's death at Megiddo.

12.   the king's servant : Benzinger has shown that this must
have been the official title of some high court functionary.   It has
been found as such upon an ancient Hebrew seal.

13.   written concerning us : read with LXX (Luc.) and
2 Chron. xxxiv. 21 'written in it.'

14.   The prophetess is described as the wife of a high court
functionary ('keeper of the wardrobe,' i.e. probably the king's),
and as one who dwelt in Jerusalem **in the second quarter** (cf.
Zeph. i. 10).   From Neh. iii. 9, 12 it would appear that the city
(exclusive of the old 'city of David' probably) was divided into
two 'districts.'   A similar arrangement may have prevailed
before the Exile.   At first sight it may seem surprising that
Jeremiah should not have been appealed to.   But Jeremiah, who
was still a young man (cf. Jer. i. 6), may not have been well

9—2

she said unto them, Thus saith the LORD, the God
of Israel : Tell ye the man that sent you unto me,
16 Thus saith the LORD, Behold, I will bring evil upon this
place, and upon the inhabitants thereof, even all the
words of the book which the king of Judah hath read :
17 because they have forsaken me, and have burned incense
unto other gods, that they might provoke me to anger
with all the work of their hands ; therefore my wrath
shall be kindled against this place, and it shall not be
18 quenched.   But unto the king of Judah, who sent you
to inquire of the LORD, thus shall ye say to him, Thus
saith the LORD, the God of Israel : As touching the
19 words which thou hast heard, because thine heart was
tender, and thou didst humble thyself before the LORD,
when thou heardest what I spake against this place, and
against the inhabitants thereof, that they should become
a desolation and a curse, and hast rent thy clothes, and
wept before me ; I also have heard thee, saith the LORD.
20 Therefore, behold, I will gather thee to thy fathers, and
thou shalt be gathered to thy grave in peace, neither
shall thine eyes see all the evil which I will bring upon
this place.   And they brought the king word again.

xxiii. 1–3.   *The covenant solemnly confirmed.*

23   And the king sent, and they gathered unto him all the
2 elders of Judah and of Jerusalem.   And the king went up

known at this time in Jerusalem, while Huldah, doubtless,
enjoyed great reputation there amongst the people, as a seer.
   15.   the man that sent you : contrast ' the king of Judah who
sent you ' (*v.* 18), which suggests the hand of a later writer.
   18.   As touching the words etc.: the original text has
simply ' the words which thou hast heard.'   Something has fallen
out.   Read with LXX (Luc.) and Vulgate : ' Inasmuch as thou
hast heard my words, and thy heart was tender' etc.
   20.   Josiah was killed in battle.   The promise, therefore,
that he should be gathered to his grave in peace was un-
fulfilled.
   xxiii. 1–3.   Before an assembly representing all classes of

to the house of the LORD, and all the men of Judah and
all the inhabitants of Jerusalem with him, and the priests,
and the prophets, and all the people, both small and great:
and he read in their ears all the words of the book of
the covenant which was found in the house of the LORD.
And the king stood by the pillar, and made a covenant 3
before the LORD, to walk after the LORD, and to keep
his commandments, and his testimonies, and his statutes,
with all *his* heart, and all *his* soul, to confirm the words
of this covenant that were written in this book: and all
the people stood to the covenant.

xxiii. 4-27. *The Deuteronomic Reformation.*

And the king commanded Hilkiah the high priest, and 4
the priests of the second order, and the keepers of the

---

the nation the king reads the words of the Law-Book, and then
solemnly enters into a covenant ' before the Lord ' to observe its
requirements. This action is confirmed by the people. The
word rendered ' covenant ' has a variety of applications in the
O.T. In the present case it denotes neither a solemn contract
between king and people (as in xi. 17), nor one between God on
the one side, the king and people on the other ; but rather a
solemn engagement, invested with high religious sanctions, on
the part of the king, and binding on the people, to keep the
injunctions of the Law-Book.

The national acceptance of a written Law-Book as the binding
religious standard was a momentous event in the history of
Israel's religion. It marked the first step towards the Judaism
of Ezra and his successors.

2. the book of the covenant: so *v.* 21. In xxii. 8, 11 the
expression used is ' book of the law.' Apparently what is meant
here is a book which forms the basis of a covenant. Cf. Ex.
xxiv. 7 (where the expression is used of an earlier body of laws).

3. by the pillar: cf. xi. 14.

4-27. The reformation of the cultus which followed the
inauguration of the covenant was of the most drastic character.
The Jerusalem Temple was purified by the removal of various
idolatrous emblems, and the high places outside Jerusalem were
suppressed. The episode about Josiah in Samaria (*vv.* 16-20) is
probably a later addition to the narrative.

4. For **the priests of the second order** read ' the second

door, to bring forth out of the temple of the LORD all
the vessels that were made for Baal, and for the Asherah,
and for all the host of heaven: and he burned them
without Jerusalem in the fields of Kidron, and carried
5 the ashes of them unto Beth-el. And he put down the
idolatrous priests, whom the kings of Judah had ordained
to burn incense in the high places in the cities of Judah,
and in the high places round about Jerusalem; them
also that burned incense unto Baal, to the sun, and to
the moon, and to the planets, and to all the host of
6 heaven. And he brought out the Asherah from the
house of the LORD, without Jerusalem, unto the brook
Kidron, and burned it at the brook Kidron, and stamped
it small to powder, and cast the powder thereof upon the
7 graves of the common people. And he brake down the
houses of the sodomites, that were in the house of the

---

priest,' i.e. the priest second in rank to the head priest; cf. xxv.
18, where the 'second priest' is mentioned as here between the
head priest and 'the keepers of the door' (or 'threshold'
margin).

Asherah is here, apparently, the name of a goddess (cf. xxi. 7
and xiii. 6 and note).

the host of heaven: cf. xxi. 3 and note.

the fields of Kidron: cf. Jer. xxxi. 40. Some scholars,
following LXX (Luc.) read 'in the lime-kilns of Kidron.'

5. the idolatrous priests: the Hebrew word *Chemarim*, so
rendered, occurs again in the O. T. only in Hos. x. 5; Zeph. i. 4.
It denotes non-Levitical idol-priests, and is always used in a dis-
paraging sense.

the planets: or, perhaps, '(heavenly) mansions,' i.e. the
zodiacal stations.

6. the graves of the common people: i.e. the common
burial place, where the poor and undistinguished were buried;
cf. Jer. xxvi. 23. The rich had family sepulchres in their own
ground.

7. the sodomites: i.e. sacred prostitutes (male and female).
Such were to be found attached to heathen sanctuaries (especially
those of Ashtoreth). This heathen accompaniment which had
invaded the Jehovah-worship (cf. Amos ii. 7; Hos. iv. 14; also
1 Kings xiv. 24) is sternly reprobated in Deut. xxiii. 18.

LORD, where the women wove hangings for the Asherah. And he brought all the priests out of the cities of Judah, 8 and defiled the high places where the priests had burned incense, from Geba to Beer-sheba; and he brake down the high places of the gates that were at the entering in of the gate of Joshua the governor of the city, which were on a man's left hand at the gate of the city. Never- 9 theless the priests of the high places came not up to the altar of the LORD in Jerusalem, but they did eat unleavened bread among their brethren. And he de- 10 filed Topheth, which is in the valley of the children of

---

hangings: the Heb. word means lit. 'houses.' Perhaps 'tunics' should be read, following LXX (Luc.).

8. The dominating idea of Deuteronomy is that the worship of Jehovah must be centralized in Jerusalem. This involved the destruction of the provincial high-places where worship had hitherto been carried on legitimately by priests of the tribe of Levi. Special provision is made for these disestablished priests in Jerusalem in Deut. xviii. 6-8, which, however, could not be carried out fully (cf. *v*. 9). Notice that Josiah brought all these priests 'out of the cities of Judah' (i.e. to Jerusalem). Geba (i.e. Geba of Benjamin, 1 Kings xv. 22) and Beersheba mark the northern and southern limits of the kingdom.

the high places of the gates: read 'the high places (or 'house,' LXX Luc.) of the satyrs' (so most moderns). For sacrifices offered to satyrs (i.e. demons in the form of he-goats) cf. Lev. xvii. 7; 2 Chron. xi. 15.

9. In spite of Deut. xviii. 6-8 the provincial priests who had been brought up to Jerusalem were not allowed to minister at the altar of the central sanctuary (it may have been found impracticable), though they were recognized as 'brethren' by the Jerusalem priesthood, and shared in their maintenance. Unleavened bread was not the normal food of the priests, as Benzinger has pointed out; it was the special food of the Passover-feast. The expression 'did eat unleavened bread among their brethren' may mean that they were recognized as 'brethren' by being allowed to participate in the Passover-feast described in *vv*. 21-23.

10. Topheth (properly *Tŏphath*) probably = 'fire-place,' on which the bodies were burned. It was placed in the 'valley of the children of Hinnom' (*Gē-hinnom* became the Gehenna of later religious terminology, cf. Matt. v. 22), the name given by Jews and Moslems to the place of future torment (Hell). By

Hinnom, that no man might make his son or his daughter
11 to pass through the fire to Molech. And he took away
the horses that the kings of Judah had given to the sun,
at the entering in of the house of the LORD, by the
chamber of Nathan-melech the chamberlain, which was
in the precincts; and he burned the chariots of the sun
12 with fire. And the altars that were on the roof of the
upper chamber of Ahaz, which the kings of Judah had
made, and the altars which Manasseh had made in the
two courts of the house of the LORD, did the king break
down, and beat *them* down from thence, and cast the
13 dust of them into the brook Kidron. And the high
places that were before Jerusalem, which were on the
right hand of the mount of corruption, which Solomon

---

most scholars this valley is identified with the *Wadi er-Rababi*
running south and west of Jerusalem. As the scene of human
sacrifices to Molech it acquired horrible associations for later
generations.

11. Probably the reference is to chariots of the sun-god
(*Shamash*) drawn by horses, a common representation in
Babylonia. For **given to** read 'set up for.' The word ren-
dered **precincts** is probably identical with 'Parbar,' which is
stated in 1 Chron. xxvi. 18 to have been on the west of the
Temple.

12. of the upper chamber of Ahaz: this clause, as the
structure of the Hebrew sentence shows, is a later gloss. The
altars referred to were on the roof of the Temple. Such altars
were erected doubtless for star-worship, which was practised
on the roofs of houses (cf. Jer. xix. 13, xxxii. 29; Zeph. i. 5).
Ahaz may have built an upper-chamber on the Temple-roof in
connexion with these altars (Benzinger).

13. The 'high places' referred to are those erected by
Solomon, as recorded in 1 Kings xi. 7, for his 'strange wives.'
'Before' = to the east of; 'on the right hand of' = to the south
of. For Ashtoreth, Chemosh, and Milcom see 1 Kings xi. 5, 7
and notes.

the mount of corruption: or 'destruction' (R.V. margin),
strictly 'the destroyer.' It is probably identical with the
southern summit of the Mount of Olives, which is now known
as the 'Mount of Offence,' a name suggested by detestation of
the idolatry practised there.

the king of Israel had builded for Ashtoreth the abomination of the Zidonians, and for Chemosh the abomination of Moab, and for Milcom the abomination of the children of Ammon, did the king defile. And he brake in pieces 14 the pillars, and cut down the Asherim, and filled their places with the bones of men. Moreover the altar that 15 was at Beth-el, and the high place which Jeroboam the son of Nebat, who made Israel to sin, had made, even that altar and the high place he brake down ; and he burned the high place and stamped it small to powder, and burned the Asherah. And as Josiah turned himself, 16 he spied the sepulchres that were there in the mount ; and he sent, and took the bones out of the sepulchres, and burned them upon the altar, and defiled it, according to the word of the LORD which the man of God proclaimed, who proclaimed these things. Then he said, 17 What monument is that which I see? And the men of

---

15. Bethel had been the chief seat of Jeroboam's bull-worship (cf. 1 Kings xii. 28 f.). It lay, of course, outside the boundaries of Josiah's kingdom.

For **and he burned the high place** read with LXX 'and he brake in pieces the stones thereof.' A 'high place,' being a mound or hill, could not be burnt.

16–20. This passage is regarded by many scholars as an interpolation. It was probably derived from a late Midrashic work which was also the source of 1 Kings xiii. 1 f. It gives an alternative and highly embellished account of the 'defiling' of Jeroboam's altar, and is inconsistent with the narrative given in *v.* 15, where the destruction of the altar is described, the existence of which is in these verses presupposed.

16. which the man of God proclaimed : some sentences have fallen out of the text immediately after this clause, which can be supplied from the LXX (Luc.). Add 'when Jeroboam stood at the feast upon the altar. And turning round he lifted up his eyes to the grave of the man of God' (who proclaimed these things etc.); cf. 1 Kings xiii. 1.

17. monument: 'yonder grave-stone.' The word occurs only twice again in the O.T., once to denote a stone erected to mark the place of an unburied body (till it should be buried : Ezek. xxxix. 15), and once of stones placed as way-marks (Jer. xxxi. 21).

the city told him, It is the sepulchre of the man of God, which came from Judah, and proclaimed these things
18 that thou hast done against the altar of Beth-el. And he said, Let him be; let no man move his bones. So they let his bones alone, with the bones of the prophet
19 that came out of Samaria. And all the houses also of the high places that were in the cities of Samaria, which the kings of Israel had made to provoke *the* LORD to anger, Josiah took away, and did to them according to
20 all the acts that he had done in Beth-el. And he slew all the priests of the high places that were there, upon the altars, and burned men's bones upon them; and he returned to Jerusalem.

21   And the king commanded all the people, saying, Keep the passover unto the LORD your God, as it is written in
22 this book of the covenant. Surely there was not kept such a passover from the days of the judges that judged Israel, nor in all the days of the kings of Israel, nor of
23 the kings of Judah; but in the eighteenth year of king Josiah was this passover kept to the LORD in Jerusalem.

---

18.   **Samaria** : i.e. the district, not the city ; cf. 1 Kings xiii. 11.

20.   This verse agrees with 1 Kings xiii. 2 (cf. also *v.* 32).

21–27.   Here the original account, broken off at *v.* 15, is resumed with a notice of the celebration of the Passover for the first time in accordance with the directions of the Law-Book (cf. Deut. xvi. 1–8).   The novelty lay in the celebration of the feast by the whole people at the central sanctuary in Jerusalem. Hitherto the passover had been sacrificed at the various local shrines ; this is now forbidden (Deut. xvi. 5).   In *v.* 25 other reforms of Josiah are briefly alluded to.   The following *v.* (26) contains some reflections by the original Deuteronomic editor ; *vv.* 26, 27 belong to the later (exilic) editorial stratum.

22.   **Surely there was not kept** etc.: render 'for there had not been kept' etc.   This celebration differed from all previous ones (see above).

23.   The express statement that the Passover was kept in the eighteenth year of king Josiah, i.e. within the same year during which the Law-Book was discovered, shows that the year was

Moreover them that had familiar spirits, and the wizards, 24
and the teraphim, and the idols, and all the abominations
that were spied in the land of Judah and in Jerusalem,
did Josiah put away, that he might confirm the words
of the law which were written in the book that Hilkiah
the priest found in the house of the LORD.   And like 25
unto him was there no king before him, that turned to
the LORD with all his heart, and with all his soul, and
with all his might, according to all the law of Moses;
neither after him arose there any like him.   Notwith- 26
standing the LORD turned not from the fierceness of his
great wrath, wherewith his anger was kindled against
Judah, because of all the provocations that Manasseh
had provoked him withal.   And the LORD said, I will 27
remove Judah also out of my sight, as I have removed
Israel, and I will cast off this city which I have chosen,
even Jerusalem, and the house of which I said, My name
shall be there.

xxiii. 28–30.   *Conclusion.*

Now the rest of the acts of Josiah, and all that he did, 28
are they not written in the book of the chronicles of the

---

reckoned from autumn, in accordance with the old Hebrew
calendar, and not from the spring.   Otherwise the Passover
would fall at the very beginning of the year, and thus not allow
time for the reformation previously described to have taken
place within the year.

24. For diviners etc. cf. xxi. 6.   All such practices are
forbidden in Deut. xviii. 9–14.   'Teraphim' (images of household gods, cf. Gen. xxxi. 19 f.; 1 Sam. xix. 13 f.) are not,
however, mentioned in Deuteronomy.

25. Notice the reflective tone of this verse, which is clearly
the work of the Deuteronomic editor, to whom the Law-Book is
'the law of Moses.'   The words 'neither after him' etc. imply
that the Judaean monarchy had come to an end, and may be
assigned to the younger editor (D²).

26, 27. Cf. xxi. 10–15.

28–30. The concluding editorial notice embodies a short account, derived, doubtless, from the Judaean annalistic document,

29 kings of Judah? In his days Pharaoh-necoh king of
  Egypt went up against the king of Assyria to the river
  Euphrates: and king Josiah went against him; and he
30 slew him at Megiddo, when he had seen him. And his
  servants carried him in a chariot dead from Megiddo,
  and brought him to Jerusalem, and buried him in his
  own sepulchre. And the people of the land took Jehoahaz
  the son of Josiah, and anointed him, and made him king
  in his father's stead.

XXIII. 31-35. JEHOAHAZ OF JUDAH (cf. 2 Chron. xxxvi. 2-4).

xxiii. 31, 32. *Introduction.*

31 Jehoahaz was twenty and three years old when he
  began to reign; and he reigned three months in Jerusalem: and his mother's name was Hamutal the daughter
32 of Jeremiah of Libnah. And he did that which was evil
  in the sight of the LORD, according to all that his fathers
  had done.

---

of Josiah's death at Megiddo. Necho II of Egypt, taking advantage of the weak condition of the Assyrian Empire, determined
to make himself master of the Syrian provinces. With this
object in view he marched to the Euphrates, but for some reason
(not stated) was opposed by Josiah at Megiddo. In the battle
Josiah was slain, and with him perished the dominating force of
the reform-movement. The battle took place probably in 608.

29. Pharaoh-necho, i.e. Necho II, reigned 609-594.

and king Josiah went against him: either as a loyal vassal
of Assyria, or because he wished to assert his absolute independence and enlarge his borders.

Megiddo: the Egyptian king came either by sea to Acco
or by the coast. In either case the most convenient place
for battle would be the broad plain of Jezreel. Consequently
Josiah marched north to Megiddo, in the plain of Jezreel, to
meet him. Herodotus (probably by mistake) locates the battle
at Magdōlos (Migdol).

when he had seen him: i.e. when they met in battle; cf.
xiv. 8.

31-35. Jehoahaz, a younger son of Josiah, as the age of his
brother, given in *v.* 36, shows, was elected king by the people,
probably because he was ready to continue the anti-Egyptian

xxiii. 33-35. *Deposition of Jehoahaz.*

And Pharaoh-necoh put him in bands at Riblah in the 33
land of Hamath, that he might not reign in Jerusalem;
and put the land to a tribute of an hundred talents of
silver, and a talent of gold. And Pharaoh-necoh made 34
Eliakim the son of Josiah king in the room of Josiah his
father, and changed his name to Jehoiakim: but he
took Jehoahaz away; and he came to Egypt, and died
there. And Jehoiakim gave the silver and the gold to 35
Pharaoh; but he taxed the land to give the money according to the commandment of Pharaoh: he exacted
the silver and the gold of the people of the land, of every
one according to his taxation, to give it unto Pharaoh-
necoh.

---

policy of his father. His short reign of three months was
terminated by Necho, who took him a prisoner to Egypt (cf.
Ezek. xix.). His brother Eliakim was made king under the
name of Jehoiakim. *vv.* 33-35 resume the annalistic document
broken off at *v.* 30.

33. **Riblah** (cf. xxv. 6 f.) lay on the Orontes at the northern
end of the Coele-Syrian plain in a position of great strategical
importance. It still bears the name. From *v.* 34 it is clear
that Necho was already marching south when it summoned
Jehoahaz to Riblah.

a talent of gold: read with LXX (Luc.), Pesh. 'ten talents
of gold.'

34. The change of name (cf. also xxiv. 17) is simply a sign
and reminder that the newly-established king is a vassal.
'Eliakim' and 'Jehoiakim' are practically identical in meaning
(='God' or 'Jehovah establishes').

and died there: cf. Jer. xxii. 10-12 (where 'Shallum'=
Jehoahaz).

35. Probably the words 'of the people of the land' (i.e. the
common people) should be deleted as an explanatory gloss on
'the land' in the first clause. They are ungrammatical in the
Hebrew text. The indemnity was raised by taxing the landed
proprietors according to their means (cf. xv. 20). The absence
of a concluding notice of the reign of Jehoahaz is remarkable.

36, 37. With the fall of Nineveh (between 608 and 606) the
power of the Assyrian Empire passed into the hands of the new
Babylonian or Chaldean dynasty, founded by Nabopolassar

XXIII. 36–XXIV. 7. JEHOIAKIM OF JUDAH.

xxiii. 36, 37. *Introduction.*

36 Jehoiakim was twenty and five years old when he began to reign; and he reigned eleven years in Jerusalem: and his mother's name was Zebidah the daughter 37 of Pedaiah of Rumah. And he did that which was evil in the sight of the LORD, according to all that his fathers had done.

xxiv. 1–4. *Jehoiakim rebels against Nebuchadrezzar.*

24 In his days Nebuchadnezzar king of Babylon came up, and Jehoiakim became his servant three years: then he 2 turned and rebelled against him. And the LORD sent against him bands of the Chaldeans, and bands of the Syrians, and bands of the Moabites, and bands of the

---

(625–605), with its capital at Babylon. One of the first acts of Nabopolassar, after the fall of Nineveh, was to reconquer the Syrian provinces which had been seized by Necho. Nebuchadnezzar (or more accurately Nebuchadrezzar), the son of Nabopolassar, inflicted a decisive defeat in 605 on the Egyptians at Carchemish (cf. Jer. xlvi. 2), one of the results of which was that Jehoiakim became the 'servant' of Nebuchadrezzar, who became king of Babylon about this time (605–604). Later, Judah rebelled, and was ultimately besieged by the Babylonians, but not till Jehoiachin had ascended the throne. While xxiv. 1 is, apparently, based on the annalistic document, xxiv. 2–5 seems to be mainly the work of the younger (exilic) editor.

xxiv. 1. This *v.* resumes the annalistic account broken off in xxiii. 35. From Jer. xxv. 1 and xlvi. 2 it appears that the fourth year of Jehoiakim synchronizes with the date of the battle of Carchemish and Nebuchadrezzar's accession.

three years : if reckoned from the first act of submission in 605, this would imply that Jehoiakim rebelled in 602, five years before the Babylonians besieged Jerusalem. Nebuchadrezzar is unlikely to have waited so long before inflicting punishment. Possibly Jehoiakim's formal submission was delayed till Syria was pacified ; in this case his rebellion would fall nearer the end of his reign.

2. For 'Syrians' probably 'Edomites' should be read (cf. xvi. 6 and note). It would seem that these predatory bands carried on a guerilla warfare against Judah till a **regular**

children of Ammon, and sent them against Judah to
destroy it, according to the word of the LORD, which he
spake by the hand of his servants the prophets. Surely 3
at the commandment of the LORD came this upon Judah,
to remove them out of his sight, for the sins of Manasseh,
according to all that he did; and also for the innocent 4
blood that he shed; for he filled Jerusalem with innocent
blood: and the LORD would not pardon.

xxiv. 5, 6 (7). *Conclusion.*

Now the rest of the acts of Jehoiakim, and all that he 5
did, are they not written in the book of the chronicles
of the kings of Judah? So Jehoiakim slept with his 6
fathers: and Jehoiachin his son reigned in his stead.
And the king of Egypt came not again any more out of 7
his land: for the king of Babylon had taken, from the
brook of Egypt unto the river Euphrates, all that pertained
to the king of Egypt.

Babylonian army could arrive. According to a remarkable
addition preserved in the LXX of 2 Chron. xxxvi. 5, these
bands, which included 'Samaritans,' were forced to retire
'according to the word of the Lord by the hand of his servants
the prophets.' Possibly a clause resembling this once stood
here, and was deleted by the compiler. This would add point
to the following verse, the first word of which ('Surely') may be
rendered 'Howbeit.'

3, 4. These verses contain the reflections of the younger
compiler. Such misfortunes were due to Jehovah's anger at
Manasseh's sins (cf. xxiii. 26 f.). For 'at the commandment of
the Lord' LXX reads 'Because of the anger of the Lord' etc.

5, 6. The 'book of the chronicles of the kings of Judah' is
here cited as a source for the last time. Some scholars suppose
that it was at about this point that the pre-exilic form of the
Books of Kings ended. The rest of the book is mainly the work
of the younger (exilic) editor. In *v.* 6 the LXX (Luc.) adds:
'and he was buried in the garden of Uzza with his father' (cf.
xxi. 18). This does not, however, accord with Jeremiah's prediction (Jer. xxii. 18–20).

7. This appended notice is, apparently, based on the
annalistic document.

XXIV. 8–17.. JEHOIACHIN OF JUDAH (cf. 2 Chron. xxxvi. 9, 10).

xxiv. 8, 9. *Introduction.*

8 Jehoiachin was eighteen years old when he began to reign ; and he reigned in Jerusalem three months : and his mother's name was Nehushta the daughter of Elna-
9 than of Jerusalem. And he did that which was evil in the sight of the LORD, according to all that his father had done.

xxiv. 10–17. *Nebuchadrezzar's first siege of Jerusalem.*

10 At that time the servants of Nebuchadnezzar king of Babylon came up to Jerusalem, and the city was be-
11 sieged.   And Nebuchadnezzar king of Babylon came
12 unto the city, while his servants were besieging it ; and Jehoiachin the king of Judah went out to the king of Babylon, he, and his mother, and his servants, and his princes, and his officers : and the king of Babylon took
13 him in the eighth year of his reign. And he carried out thence all the treasures of the house of the LORD, and the treasures of the king's house, and cut in pieces all

---

8–17. Jehoiakim died just in time to escape the vengeance of Nebuchadrezzar, which fell on Jehoiachin.   The latter king's brief reign of three months was marked by the siege and surrender of Jerusalem and the first deportation of its inhabitants. The king, with his court and the aristocracy, and skilled artisans—all the best elements of the population—were carried into captivity to Babylon. Among the captives was the prophet Ezekiel, who foresaw, and consistently predicted, the downfall of the weakened remnant that was left under the rule of Zedekiah. This first captivity took place in 598 or 597 ; the final destruction of the city in 587.

10. The siege was apparently begun before the arrival of Nebuchadrezzar in person.

12.   went out : i.e. surrendered ; cf. xviii. 31.

the eighth year etc. : as Nebuchadrezzar did not complete the first year of his reign till 604, his eighth year would fall in 597 ; but the year, according to xxv. 27, must be 598. Possibly both here and in xxv. 8, 605 was reckoned the first year of Nebuchadrezzar. Jeremiah lii. 28 gives the seventh year of Nebuchadrezzar (= 598).

13, 14. These verses, which speak of all the treasures of the

the vessels of gold which Solomon king of Israel had made in the temple of the LORD, as the LORD had said. And he carried away all Jerusalem, and all the princes, 14 and all the mighty men of valour, even ten thousand captives, and all the craftsmen and the smiths; none remained, save the poorest sort of the people of the land. And he carried away Jehoiachin to Babylon; and the 15 king's mother, and the king's wives, and his officers, and the chief men of the land, carried he into captivity from Jerusalem to Babylon. And all the men of might, even 16 seven thousand, and the craftsmen and the smiths a thousand, all of them strong and apt for war, even them the king of Babylon brought captive to Babylon. And 17 the king of Babylon made Mattaniah his father's brother king in his stead, and changed his name to Zedekiah.

---

city and Temple being carried off, and *all* Jerusalem going into captivity, appear to be out of place. The greater part of the treasures was only carried away in 587, when the city and Temple were destroyed and the remnant of the population deported. Probably the verses are a fragment relating to the events of 587, which has been misplaced. Notice that 'thence' in *v.* 13 has no antecedent in the preceding narrative.

14. the poorest sort etc.: an excellent description of the population of Jerusalem *after* the first deportation.

15. For the captivity of Jehoiachin and the queen-mother cf. Jer. xxii. 24-27.

16. men of might : perhaps = 'men of wealth' here.

strong etc.: this clause refers to all the classes previously mentioned. All were able-bodied men who could fight. By deporting all these elements of strength Nebuchadrezzar hoped to make further resistance impossible.

17. For the change of name cf. xxiii. 34 and note.

xxiv. 18-xxv. 21. The only events here recorded of the eleven years' reign of the last king of Judah are those in connexion with the siege and destruction of Jerusalem, which happened in 587 or 586. We learn from Jeremiah (cf. xxvii. f.) that an anti-Babylonian party, which was constantly involved in the web of Egyptian intrigue, was powerful quite early in Zedekiah's reign. Later the unfortunate king was influenced by this party to commit the state to a policy of open rebellion. Jerusalem, however, offered a most stubborn resistance, when it was at length invested by a Babylonian army, and was only reduced

XXIV. 18–XXV. 21.   Zedekiah of Judah (cf. 2 Chron.
xxxvi. 11–23).

xxiv. 18–20 a.   *Introduction.*

18   Zedekiah was twenty and one years old when he began
to reign; and he reigned eleven years in Jerusalem: and
his mother's name was Hamutal the daughter of Jeremiah
19 of Libnah.   And he did that which was evil in the sight
of the LORD, according to all that Jehoiakim had done.
20 For through the anger of the LORD did it come to pass
in Jerusalem and Judah, until he had cast them out from
his presence:

xxiv. 20b–xxv. 21.   *Destruction of the State and second deportation to Babylon.*

25 and Zedekiah rebelled against the king of Babylon.   And
it came to pass in the ninth year of his reign, in the tenth
month, in the tenth day of the month, that Nebuchadnezzar king of Babylon came, he and all his army, against
Jerusalem, and encamped against it; and they built forts
2 against it round about.   So the city was besieged unto
3 the eleventh year of king Zedekiah.   On the ninth day
of the *fourth* month the famine was sore in the city, so
4 that there was no bread for the people of the land.   Then

---

after a siege of 18 months.   Even then Zedekiah and his army
succeeded in breaking through the Chaldean lines, but were
overtaken and captured.   The city was razed to the ground and
the population deported.   The parallel accounts in Jer. xxxix. 1,
2, 4 and lii. were probably extracted from Kings, but often preserve a purer text.

18.   Jehoahaz and Zedekiah were sons of the same mother (cf.
xxiii. 31), and therefore full brothers.

xxv. 1.   With the Babylonian calendar, which reckoned the
beginning of the year in spring, came in the numbering of the
months (first, second etc.).   The siege was begun in the tenth
month (= January) of Zedekiah's ninth year (= 588 or 587), and
the city was taken in the fourth month (= July) of his eleventh
year (= 587 or 586).

3.   For the famine see Jer. xxxvii. 21, xxxviii. 9.

a breach was made in the city, and all the men of war *fled* by night by the way of the gate between the two walls, which was by the king's garden: (now the Chaldeans were against the city round about:) and *the king* went by the way of the Arabah. But the army of the 5 Chaldeans pursued after the king, and overtook him in the plains of Jericho: and all his army was scattered from him. Then they took the king, and carried him 6 up unto the king of Babylon to Riblah; and they gave judgement upon him. And they slew the sons of Zede- 7 kiah before his eyes, and put out the eyes of Zedekiah, and bound him in fetters, and carried him to Babylon.

Now in the fifth month, on the seventh day of the 8 month, which was the nineteenth year of king Nebuchadnezzar, king of Babylon, came Nebuzaradan the captain of the guard, a servant of the king of Babylon, unto Jerusalem: and he burnt the house of the LORD, and the 9 king's house; and all the houses of Jerusalem, even

---

4. and all the men of war *fled* etc.: read 'and when the king and all the men of war saw it, they fled and went out of the city by night' etc.

between the two walls: cf. Is. xxii. 11. A point on the S.E. side of the city is meant, at the mouth of the Tyropoean valley. Possibly the west wall of the eastern hill and the east wall of the western hill ran parallel to each other, for some distance up the Tyropoean, and the space between them is referred to (Benzinger).

the Arabah: i.e. the depression of the Jordan valley.

5. For **was scattered** read 'had been scattered,' i.e. they had already dispersed in the open country.

6. For Riblah see xxiii. 33 and note. Read 'he gave' for 'they gave' (Jer. lii. 9).

7. Jer. lii. 11 adds: 'and put him in prison till the day of his death.'

8. the nineteenth year: i.e. 586. But according to Jeremiah lii. 29 the year was the 18th of Nebuchadrezzar, i.e. 587. See on xxiv. 12 and xxv. 27.

9. Not only the Temple and palace but **all the houses of Jerusalem** are burnt (the following clause 'even every great house' must be an incorrect gloss). This was done apparently

10 every great house, burnt he with fire. And all the army
of the Chaldeans, that were *with* the captain of the
guard, brake down the walls of Jerusalem round about.
11 And the residue of the people that were left in the city,
and those that fell away, that fell to the king of Babylon,
and the residue of the multitude, did Nebuzaradan the
12 captain of the guard carry away captive. But the captain
of the guard left of the poorest of the land to be vine-
13 dressers and husbandmen. And the pillars of brass that
were in the house of the LORD, and the bases and the
brasen sea that were in the house of the LORD, did the
Chaldeans break in pieces, and carried the brass of them
14 to Babylon. And the pots, and the shovels, and the
snuffers, and the spoons, and all the vessels of brass
15 wherewith they ministered, took they away. And the
firepans, and the basons; that which was of gold, in
gold, and that which was of silver, in silver, the captain
16 of the guard took away. The two pillars, the one sea,
and the bases, which Solomon had made for the house
of the LORD; the brass of all these vessels was without
17 weight. The height of the one pillar was eighteen cubits,
and a chapiter of brass was upon it: and the height of

---

by express orders sent (after some delay) direct from Nebuchadrezzar.

11. This verse states that the entire population of Jerusalem,
without exception, was deported, including those who had
deserted to the Babylonians ('fell away') during the siege. For
the residue of the multitude Jer. lii. 15 has (correctly) 'the
residue of the artificers' (R.V. marg.).

12. In the rural districts outside Jerusalem only **the poorest,**
i.e. those without landed property, were left 'to be vinedressers
and husbandmen.'

13-15. These verses enumerate various furniture and utensils
of the Temple and describe how they were dealt with by the
Babylonians. The larger ones were broken up and the metal sent
to Babylon.

16, 17. The full text of this passage can be seen in Jer. lii.
21-23. It gives a more exact description of the pillars and
bases already mentioned in *v.* 13. It seems to have been

the chapter was three cubits; with network and pomegranates upon the chapter round about, all of brass: and like unto these had the second pillar with network. And the captain of the guard took Seraiah the chief 18 priest, and Zephaniah the second priest, and the three keepers of the door: and out of the city he took an 19 officer that was set over the men of war; and five men of them that saw the king's face, which were found in the city; and the scribe, the captain of the host, which mustered the people of the land; and threescore men of the people of the land, that were found in the city. And Nebuzaradan the captain of the guard took them, 20 and brought them to the king of Babylon to Riblah. And the king of Babylon smote them, and put them to 21 death at Riblah in the land of Hamath. So Judah was carried away captive out of his land.

---

extracted from an old document which described the Temple furniture, and originally had no connexion with the history of the destruction by the Babylonians. In *v.* 17 correct **three cubits** to 'five cubits,' as in Jer. lii. 22.

18–21. A number of important officials, who were taken prisoners in the city, are sent to Riblah for execution.

18. For these five heads of the Temple hierarchy cf. xxiii. 4.

19. **an officer**: 'a certain eunuch' (marg.).

five...that saw the king's face: i.e. from the king's immediate *entourage*. The number given in Jeremiah is *seven*.

the scribe etc.: read as in Jer. 'the secretary of the captain of the host.'

21. **was carried...captive**: 'went into exile.' Jer. lii. 28–30 appends a list of the numbers of Judaeans deported at various times by Nebuchadrezzar.

22–26. This passage is a short summary based upon the narrative given in Jer. xxxix. 11–xliii. 7. It may be the work of the younger editor. It is not included in Jer. lii.

The work of pacification in the desolated land was entrusted to Gedaliah, a Judaean noble and a friend of the prophet Jeremiah. He succeeded in inducing the scattered bands to come in and make their submission; but his work was ruined by the insane action of a member of the Davidic house, Ishmael, who assassinated the Governor and some Chaldean soldiers who were with him. In terror of the consequences, the heads of the

XXV. 22–26. GEDALIAH GOVERNOR OF JUDAH.

22 And as for the people that were left in the land of Judah, whom Nebuchadnezzar king of Babylon had left, even over them he made Gedaliah the son of Ahikam, the son of Shaphan, governor.

23 Now when all the captains of the forces, they and their men, heard that the king of Babylon had made Gedaliah governor, they came to Gedaliah to Mizpah, even Ishmael the son of Nethaniah, and Johanan the son of Kareah, and Seraiah the son of Tanhumeth the Netophathite, and Jaazaniah the son of the Maacathite, they 24 and their men. And Gedaliah sware to them and to their men, and said unto them, Fear not because of the servants of the Chaldeans: dwell in the land, and serve 25 the king of Babylon, and it shall be well with you. But it came to pass in the seventh month, that Ishmael the son of Nethaniah, the son of Elishama, of the seed royal,

---

small Judaean community fled to Egypt, compelling the aged prophet Jeremiah, in spite of his protests, to accompany them (cf. Jer. xliii. 7).

22. Gedaliah's father Ahikam had befriended Jeremiah (cf. Jer. xxvi. 24), and was one of the deputation sent to consult the prophetess Huldah when the law-book was discovered (cf. 2 Kings xxii. 12). Both father and son were doubtless members of the moderate party, led by Jeremiah, who discountenanced a war-like policy. Gedaliah was, therefore, well fitted to undertake the difficult task of pacification assigned to him.

23. captains of the forces: i.e. those in command of the scattered armed bands, which had not yet surrendered to the Chaldeans. Possibly they were the remnants of the Jerusalem garrison that had broken out of the city under Zedekiah.

Mizpah: the modern *En-Nebī Samwīl*, the highest point near Jerusalem, a little to the west of the city.

Ishmael: the traitor, who, in league with the king of Ammon, compassed the assassination of Gedaliah (cf. Jer. xl. 14).

24. Read 'Fear not to serve the Chaldeans,' as in Jer. xl. 9.

25. in the seventh month: i.e. of the year of the destruction of the city.

came, and ten men with him, and smote Gedaliah, that
he died, and the Jews and the Chaldeans that were with
him at Mizpah. And all the people, both small and **26**
great, and the captains of the forces, arose, and came
to Egypt: for they were afraid of the Chaldeans.

XXV. 27–30. THE RELEASE OF JEHOIACHIN (cf. Jer. lii.
31–34).

And it came to pass in the seven and thirtieth year of **27**
the captivity of Jehoiachin king of Judah, in the twelfth
month, on the seven and twentieth day of the month,
that Evil-merodach king of Babylon, in the year that
he began to reign, did lift up the head of Jehoiachin king
of Judah out of prison ; and he spake kindly to him, and **28**
set his throne above the throne of the kings that were

27–30. The feeling that a book should not end on a note of
unrelieved gloom is strongly marked in post-exilic Judaism.
Some feeling of this kind may have led to the insertion of the
present section, which recounts how the lot of the captive
Jehoiachin—who, indeed, was still the legitimate king of Judah—
was ameliorated in exile. On the death of Nebuchadrezzar in
562, the Judaean king was liberated and treated with marked
favour at the Babylonian court during the rest of his life. A
pious Jew writing during the Exile might well look upon this as
a sign that Jehovah's favour had not been entirely withdrawn
from the dynasty of David and as the harbinger of a more
fortunate future. The final edition of Kings was probably
completed soon after Jehoiachin's death.

27. Nebuchadrezzar died in 562, and the present passage
states that it was towards the end of the last month of this year
that Jehoiachin was released. This would be in the spring of
the year 561, according to our reckoning (the Babylonian year
begins in spring). If the 37 years are added to 561, the result
is 598 as the date of the first captivity (not 597). At this time
Jehoiachin would be 18 + 37 = 55 years old.

Evil-merodach, Bab. *Amil-Marduk* (i.e. 'man of Marduk '),
reigned from 562 to 560. The favour he had shown to the
Jewish king was, apparently, continued by his successors. For
' did lift up the head ' cf. Gen. xl. 13.

28. set his throne etc.: i.e. gave him precedence over other
captive kings at court ' by allowing him a higher chair of state
in the royal hall. So Cyrus kept Croesus king of Lydia at his
Court ' (Ball).

29 with him in Babylon. And he changed his prison garments, and did eat bread before him continually all the
30 days of his life. And for his allowance, there was a
continual allowance given him of the king, every day a
portion, all the days of his life.

---

29. He became a regular guest at the royal table ; cf. 1 Kings
ii. 7.

INDEX

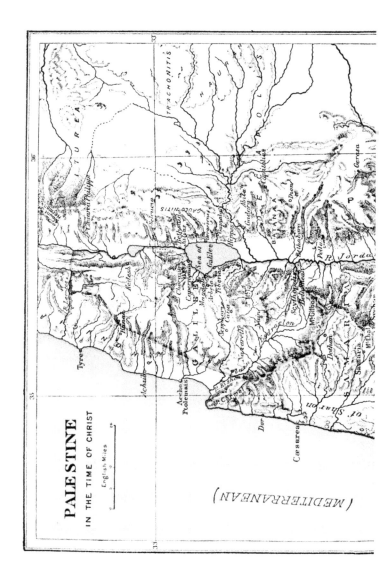

PALESTINE

IN THE TIME OF CHRIST

English Miles

(MEDITERRANEAN)

CAMB. UNIV. PRESS.

Copyright